Letters to Nowhere

(Second Edition)

Royce Levi

Letters to Nowhere

Copyright © 2010 Royce Levi

A copy of this publication can be found in the National Library
of Australia.

ISBN: 9781921791482 (pbk.)

Published by Book Pal
www.bookpal.com.au

*For the children of many lands who
have filled my classes for all these years*

NOTE ON THE
SECOND EDITION

The publishers wish to point out that all letters from the first volume of *Letters to Nowhere* have been included in the Second Edition, with one addition.

The reasons for the addition will become apparent to the reader on completion of the text.

Each letter is an unedited, primary source.

We also wish to thank most sincerely, participating government departments, universities, and their employees for their support and cooperation in the development and verification of these materials for publication.

Special thanks are also due to Dr L. Mustikos for a vital and significant contribution to this second edition.

* * * * *

Photographs and Art Work
S. J. Cavell

All photographs were taken in Australian locations by S. J. Cavell. They have been added to the text by Dr Cavell, editorially, with selected quotations from the letters, as a compassionate and respectful tribute to the original author.

* * * * *

The mind is its own place, and in itself
Can make a Heav'n of Hell, a Hell of Heav'n.

— Milton : *Paradise Lost*

* * * * *

"Give me your tired, your poor,
Your huddled masses yearning to breathe free,
The wretched refuse of your teeming shore.
Send these, the homeless, tempest-tossed to me,
I lift my lamp beside the golden door!"

From the sonnet "The New Colossus" by Emma Lazarus, on the pedestal of the Statue of Liberty

* * * * *

An Unfrequented Verse

Beneath our radiant Southern Cross
We'll toil with hearts and hands;
To make this Commonwealth of ours
Renowned of all the lands;
For those who've come across the seas
We've boundless plains to share;
With courage let us all combine
To advance Australia fair.
In joyful strains then let us sing,
Advance Australia fair.

* * * * *

The Universal Declaration of Human Rights

The General Assembly of the United Nations:
December 10, 1948.

Article 11:

(2) No one shall be held guilty of any penal offence on account of any act or omission which did not constitute a penal offence, under national or international law, at the time when it was committed.

Contents

First Contact

RETURN ADDRESS

Detention Officer 106
Internment Pty Ltd
PO Box 313
Rampart SA 5813
Australia

26 January 2003

Dr Samuel Cavell
Executive Editor
Universal Publishing
Circular Quay, Sydney
New South Wales, 2000, Australia

Dear Dr Cavell,

I am sending you this bundle of letters in an effort to gain advice from you. They may be worth publishing. I figure your organisation is my best bet because of your well-known original, non-fiction publications. If you can help, it will be much appreciated.

<u>Background: How I Came to Have the Letters</u>

It was one of those days out there in the broken, dusty countryside where I work, when the sun forgot to set. Instead of sleeping, the hot-to-trot old lover boy decided to have it off with the sky and produced an orgasm of colour which made the discos of my young days look like a black and white movie. He lingered on, that sun, holding on like one of my own kids clinging to his favourite toy in a fight with another kid, but in this case simply refusing to let the day go.

Somehow when that day finally died, I had a feeling that things were strangely off centre in my workplace. The light had almost faded completely when they allowed me into that vacant cell. There it was, empty as a Siberian ice chest in winter. Strange to see, because the old refugee had lived in it for so long.

Nothing was left of the old fellow but a shrivelled toilet bag and a pair of tattered slippers. Now there was the odd thing. I was so used to seeing signs of this man's existence in that cramped cell: scraps of paper, worn out pens lying on the floor, battered books in his God-forsaken foreign language. Something was not right about the emptiness of the old codger's room.

He had always been the shifty one of my rounds. A strange, ancient bird with a rambling, piercing eye. Long white hair and sweeping beard, like a character from the *Tales of the Arabian Nights* my mother used to read to me.

They say, when he first came to the place, he caused all Hell to break loose. He scratched peace signs on walls and pavements with a stone he found in the exercise yard. For every day of his first few months, at exercise time, he sat in the middle of the yard and did a Buddhist chant for hours on end until finally they refused to let him out of his cell. When they did that, he went on a hunger strike for a week until they put him back into the yard, whereupon he immediately stopped chanting.

After this wild early time, he seemed to settle down. He just took to meditating. Standing like a statue in the yard, his beard the only thing moving, day after day for hours watching time go by.

Perhaps, before I go on, I should explain my occupation. I am, you might say, a minder of refugees. You have probably heard of my workplace. It's an internment-centre you'll find stuck in the dusty, desert plains of Australia. I won't give it a name in case that gets me into trouble, but you'll find it easily if you look. The name doesn't really matter anyway.

The fact is, this centre does exist in a very remote area of the Australian inland. Two reasons for this remoteness: one, escape is not a practical option for refugees; and two, out of sight, out of public criticism.

Not a line of work to write home about, mine. I'm really another kind of prison guard and the people I control are a pretty sorry lot. Boat people. Queue jumpers. Law-breakers. What a shifty bunch! Hard to talk to. Rambling eyes. Broken English.

Still, it's a job. A uniform and meals. I'm not qualified for much else. And it's not all that hard because you have all the power. You have your ups and downs, but it's OK. Sometimes they have fits of disobedience. Refuse to eat. Climb onto a roof and stay there, shouting things I do not understand. Even stitch up their lips. But you win in the end.

The place is crowded now too. Intended originally for 400. The numbers got up to 1500. We even had children--God Almighty--up to 456 kids at the one time--staying for on average one year, eight months and eleven days --watching the riots--the suicides--even trying to kill themselves. Worries me a lot. Sometimes. But although I read a lot and think a lot, my future's not educated safe. What other job can I do?

We guards have to work hard. We are pretty fit and well trained for physical situations. The company teaches us pretty good control skills before we get the job. Any one who takes us on and gives us trouble, in the end is likely to come off second best.

I must confess we are a bit rough at times. But how can you avoid it? Life is rarely a Sunday-school picnic these days.

Anyway, my job on this occasion was not to fight or keep order. It was simply to get the cell ready for the next occupant. When I came to work in the morning I discovered that the old man was no longer there.

Nobody warned me he was going. And no one told me where he had gone. It was all very hush-hush and organised by higher authorities. But that departure was very sudden. Why was he here one day and gone the next? Disappeared without a trace? Well no. That's not exactly right . . .

After signing some forms and a bit of discussion, in I went with a mop, a bucket, a broom and dust pan, as the winter evening settled down. There was the empty cell. There were his few pathetic trifles on the bed.

Something was wrong. After all the years he was locked up there, and all the meetings you had with him, you got to know from those dark eyes, that there was more to him than the usual surface stuff. That's why this time I kept looking for more.

There were rumours about him too. Him and his silent, knowing ways. His background was a mystery and he had this odd smile on his pale, bearded face most of the time. After his spectacular start, management suspected him.

They bugged his cubicle. Wired me from time to time so I could ask leading questions. Left his light on for a week or two to give him a chance to crack. Always with the usual excuse of 'in the name of security'. Fear of terrorism. They kept after him for years but we found nothing dangerous or incriminating. What we saw was what we got.

I got to know him better after a while. Actually, I'm not much younger myself. I've well and truly said goodbye to fifty.

He rarely talked for long periods. And when he did, it was usually to me. I was his one real contact with the centre's guards. We met most days anyway, when I was on duty.

Sometimes we got on quite well. Just a few words normally when necessary in his foreign language and broken English. He seemed to speak more than one language. He was a very strange bird. Now I realise I might have told him some things I wish I hadn't.

That was definitely why the emptiness of his lockup after he had gone unsettled me. Very strange. Very, very strange.

I kept looking around. And around. You know what I mean?

On top of what I have been saying, somehow because he knew me pretty well and often seemed to see through me, I think he figured I would find these letters in the end. He used to say, 'You get me out of here, I give you present.' We would both laugh. But I can still remember now, the twinkle in his eye.

In no time at all, on this particular day, I became convinced that cell was too empty. Something in the room was out of place. Something was missing.

I used to be a builder you know. I knew bricks and mortar. A bit of the wall attracted my attention. Funny unevenness.

All at once there it was. One of the bricks in the corner behind the bed moved when I touched it. That was how I found it. In that exposed and well-guarded cell he had made for himself a private cavity. And in that space I found this bundle of letters, carefully wrapped in a piece of grubby cloth and bound by a strip of grimy rag.

When I opened the bundle it really knocked me over. The writing was in perfect English. I couldn't believe it. I had spent all those years trying to talk to him in bits and pieces of English, which was my job and which I was not very good at it, when out of the blue I discovered this.

Often during all our conversations, I used to feel he was just laughing at me; playing a game with me. We struggled to grab meanings which I suspected he knew all the time. And now, after he is gone, I find the mysterious old bastard writes perfect English.

I get the feeling he had a dark past. In his other life maybe he was a diplomat, or a secret agent. He was obviously fleeing from something. Some danger or other. Yet from his letters, you can see he had a conscience too. And he obviously suffered a lot during his life.

No doubt about it, it was weird. Very weird. Way beyond me.

That's it then. Here are the letters. I am rather relieved to pass them on to you.

Nobody will tell me what really happened to the old man. Was he some kind of dangerous political prisoner they had to deport secretly, you know--a spy come in from the cold?

Did he finally decide to end all his suffering and hang himself in despair from the ceiling, forcing them to slip his body away to cover up the mess of his death? Or did they forget to close his door on purpose, so that he could wander off to freedom and die in the desert?

Who was this old fellow really? Did he know dangerous things about important people? Was he an undercover man who had the goods on powerful governments and agencies? Maybe he was a non-existent terrorist; you know, a kind of weapon of mass destruction like the ones which help the politicians I've been voting for go to war and win elections.

Who knows? Anyway, he's gone. Disappeared. Beamed up to somewhere else. Now we'll never know.

The letters too. I've just finished reading them. They are highly strange. I really find them highly strange.

That's why now you've got them. That's why I want to get you to have a look at them and tell me what you think? You and your organisation are more likely to be able to sort all this out than a ham-fisted internment-centre guard like me. Perhaps they should become a book.

By the way, we have absolutely no details of family or social background for this man. His slate is completely blank. In fact he seems to have been a complete loner all his life.

That's another thing that has got me puzzled. His past is such a vacuum that it occurred to me maybe this girl he writes to might just be a figment of his imagination. You know. A kind of defence against madness. Who knows? I don't. People do funny things when they are shut off from their branch of the human race.

In the meantime, I'll be there to resume my duties
tomorrow. I look forward to your reply. I'll be really
glad to hear your ideas when you are ready.

Yours sincerely
Herbert Clinker (Not his real name)

* * * * *

The Letters To Laura

I

Alone

The world is but a little place after all.
— English Proverb

Dearest Laura,
Child of My Memories,

Here in this prison I am not a person but a number. All the people here are merely numbers. To be an illegal immigrant has become the darkest of infamies.

But numbers do not breathe and fear and love and hate and dare to be different. Only people can do those things and then tell their own stories.

You would not know me now my child. Time and place can bring far-reaching changes.

This empty universe with wires around it where I am now confined is more than just another space. It is a place of aggressive isolation. A heartless concoction of barbed entanglements which sometimes I try to climb and find blood on my hands, although I have harmed no one.

I have been a prisoner here now for many years. Only through great effort today do I dream of freedom.

It is hard to be listened to here. The words I speak are mostly blown away by the wind. My only true audience is you. You are still very close to me. So close, I can see my smile reflected in your eyes whenever I choose.

When I think of you, your spirit seizes mine and somehow I am free. Free of the pain they have given me. Of the disdain. Of this unremitting enclosure. Of the imposed ritual. Of the sameness of measured days.

Even though agony rules my life now and the loneliness hangs over me, I still have you. So my only salvation is to write to you.

Dearest Laura, the mind is another place. It is the only region where we are truly free. That is why I must escape through my mind and tell you the stories I hear.

You are a flower in my garden of recollection. A garden is a scene of difference not uniformity. That is one of the secrets of its beauty. Every flower of every shape and colour adds something to the whole. So I will tell you tales I have found in my garden as if they were picked flowers.

My letters will be but butterflies' wings ever so faintly influencing the wind. But nevertheless some day that wind may become a tempest.

I know in my heart that I will eventually leave this place and wander among the wild flowers. When that will be I cannot tell. Last night I dreamt that would happen not in weeks, months or years but in days. But dreams are only pretending, aren't they?

Even so, perhaps sooner than they can know, M0131 will be gone from this place. Some day.

As for my enemies, endings are later than they think.

Grow tall, my other beloved flower.

Your loving Narni,
M0131.

When Freedom Turns to Shadows

II

Stay

A friend is another self.

— Aristotle

Coelum non animum mutant qui trans mare currunt.
Those who cross the sea change the sky but not themselves.

— Horace: *Epistles*

Dearest Laura With The Smiling Face,

Torture came again today. Some torture of the body-- yes, but also torture of the mind, the worst kind of all -- intrusive suffering.

I have become a stranger in a strange land. To be an alien is the harshest of destinies. You are an eternal object of suspicion. A danger in everything you do. A convenient distraction from darker secrets. It is never an easy fate.

Thoughts in this place are mad contrivances which capture your mind and makeyoumakeyoumakeyou climb the slippery walls in vain to find a way out, and look for escape in tubes where you cannot move, and under blankets where you cannot breathe, and in the fetid water of drains where you have no footing.

You cannot dig yourself out of a wire cage when your only tools are your fingernails. You cannot cut your mind out of your body with a scalpel. Or can you?

No fancy clothes here either. Instead we are drenched in uniformity. Numbers and grey garb which have a dehumanising effect. That was the concentration camp tactic wasn't it?

I do miss you especially, but I would not want you here where the sun throws barbed wire shadows onto the ground. Where the night refuses to promise you a better day and where you can see the stars only if you stand on the tips of your toes in your cell.

All the people who are here wish they were not, except those who are paid to make sure you do not leave. Yet with every thought of you, I leave this place and wander amidst the fun of our past togetherness.

Although you are now a beautiful young woman, yet in many ways you are still a child to me. You are part of my story.

Do you remember the smells of our teeming city and our walks by the solitary sea? Do you recall the magic we made together? Me, the old man and you the child who believed in me.

Do you remember when I made pennies disappear and re-appear in your ear? When you listened to my tales of adventure and held your breath in wonder that I had been to so many places? Where people walked upside down on the other side of the world without falling off and traipsed backwards so as not to be lost? Do you remember?

Do you remember when those waves from the sea chased us up the sand and tried to bite our toes? We were not afraid were we? And then we heard the voices in the shells telling us to come back to the sea.

And on that cloudy day I lost my shadow and you lost yours. We could not find them, no matter how hard we tried.

Can you recall when we told a funny story to that monkey in the zoo and he couldn't stop laughing? Your company was the very essence of life. Now I have nothing but your absence.

But enough of that unhappiness. You are my peace. You deserve another story or two to pass the time.

I must tell you the tales of the companions I have here in this barren place. People like me who have been imprisoned for being from elsewhere. Somehow such people find each other and a piece of their solitude ends. You have to work to find the stories however. It is like crossing to another galaxy sometimes.

But their stories give me peace. That is why, more than anything else, I must tell them to you. I know you love to listen to my tales.

* * * * *

I have found one brother here. An old man just like me who lived within these fences far away from you, but without a loving child with a smiling face. No one to write a letter to. He longed for someone to share his experiences and then he found me. He has this story. The history of M1359 and his dog. . .

Once upon the memory of a smile, dearest Laura, M1359 lived a happy life far away from this barren land. Many things around him brought laughter into his eyes. He loved his work making beautiful chairs, tables and other charming things.

He had many friends, a loving wife and a daughter very much like you. And a dog, Drago, who endlessly played with pieces of his cast-off wood.

Happiness seemed to M1359 a normal part of life. Even the birds in the large tree of his garden were willing to share his joy. Sadness did not exist in his world.

Until one terrible day. The suddenness splintered his mind. He was walking carefree beyond the shadow of a big maple as the town-hall clock struck eleven. The white tower glistened in the morning sunshine as the first chimes rang out.

On the seventh stroke, the tower disappeared in a ball of fire and hellish smoke. There followed a storm of sound and a revolution of explosions and acrid fumes. Sarajevo erupted.

M1359 was hurled from his feet and blown along the street like tumbleweed in the wind. As he struggled to stand and peered through the chaos, he realised he was a witness to the start of a war.

The explosions continued as he ran through the turmoil towards his home. After several painful minutes he arrived there to find only his dazed dog crying beside the wreckage of his shattered white fence.

The remains of his life--everyone and everything he loved--had disappeared into a chasm of dust and debris and acrid fumes. There was nothing but a crater and rubble where once his home stood. He knew at once that his wife and child were dead.

The air around him coughed up smoke.

His mind for a moment floated off into the past. His wife was kissing him again. Passionately, as if it was their first kiss. Once more he found himself lying in that bed with her wondrous, warm body enfolding him. O the softness. And those eyes, below him looking up at him lovingly with such beguiling light, smiling, enticing . . . with no need for words.

Then his mind shifted. Can you picture him Laura? Once again holding out his arms, this time to a little girl looking across the garden at him. There she is again with her long, flowing, curly hair. Daddy's little girl, now with arms around the neck of the big dog who, as always, stoically endures the little girl's embrace.

Gone. Gone now. All except the dog.

Can you understand what it is like in one slash of time to discover war? War, a turmoil triggered by festering hatreds which turn neighbours and friends into reviled enemies.

The shells continued to fall around him as he took the dog in his arms and started to run. Safety was non-existent so he didn't stop until he found apparent shelter under a shattered bridge beside the river. There he regained his breath, hugging the dog and rocking to and fro to the percussive rhythm of the barrage around him.

The explosions continued throughout the day and into the night. When the morning came, M1359 and Drago emerged into the relative calm of intermittent gunfire and threaded their way through a ruined city back to a home that wasn't there.

A few other survivors lurched dazedly into that shattered street, but their words had died with their loved ones, to be replaced by compassionate glances and unstructured cries of bereavement. Their world was now transformed. Things as well as humans die in a war.

Drago seemed to feel the sadness as much as his master. He looked at M1359 with big, dark eyes brimming with sadness and leaned towards him. The man put his arms around his dog and they stayed together, fixed in their own eerie silence as the turmoil thundered around them.

* * * * *

Four days later and a hundred miles away from where the battle still raged, a man and a dog could be seen walking around the shadowy wharves of an ancient port. The man was dressed in distressed clothes and walked slowly, with his head bent and his body leaning forward under the burden of an insignificant haversack, the dog loyally following at his heels.

The man was M1359. He had stayed in his destroyed neighbourhood long enough to bury his loved ones. When it was done, he had thrust a few clothes into a bag, taken from the ruins of his house the strong money tin he had kept in happier times, and snatched some bones for his dog. He left then, without looking back.

If you watched him carefully now, you would see him look anxiously behind him. Then you would see him join a crowd of furtive figures slipping silently aboard a rusty and battered vessel, moored unobtrusively in the shadows of a larger ship.

These were his latest steps in a desperate escape. Now he was a different man. He was a fugitive. A danger to decent people. A person to be questioned. Pitilessly. A suspicious stranger everywhere but in his shattered homeland.

'No animals,' said the captain of the boat. 'People not dogs.' Even though he gave the boatman all his money for his passage, nothing would persuade that sea-scarred man to give Drago a place on board. So M1359 climbed the steps back to the wharf and left his dog sitting there with some decaying flesh on bones.

'Stay! Stay there. Stay!' he said with reluctant venom.

In a very short time the boat set off into the night, leaving the dog on the wharf watching its departure path across the moonlit waters. M1359 could just make out the dog's dark figure, head held high and watching. Watching. You could almost see those eyes straining towards the departing vessel.

Suddenly, to his horror, the master saw his dog leap into the water. 'No! No!' M1359 cried. 'Go back! No! No! Go Back!' But his words were drowned in the waves.

This time, the dog refused to be obedient. He paddled after the boat into the night.

When morning came, in the very first light, the desperate man strained his eyes looking for his one remaining friend. But the vessel's wake, stretching as far as the horizon, was a blemish on an empty sea. Not a trace of the dog remained.

M1359 suddenly felt old and infinitely alone. Yet here he was in that leaking boat crowded with people.

The beleaguered craft struggled on. Winds sprang up and at times it was barely afloat. Days wrestled into more days until the ancient vessel had almost reached this land where now I live.

In the end, Laura, the sea decides whether or not sailors deserve to reach their destination. The waves in this case seemed to be furious with these intruders for using such a decrepit means of transport. Just as the journey was about to end, the boat sank.

M1359 survived by clutching a floating plank. There were not enough planks so many of the other boatpeople drowned. He was rescued by some kind fishermen. They gave him some clothes, food to go and a little local money.

He thanked them and walked off into the emptiness of a strange land. He spent a year or two hiding in the back blocks until he was arrested.

He had no papers. No money. People did not trust him. They did not believe his story for which he had no evidence. Pity for an alien was unthinkable. Thus he was brought to this place of detention, my home for these years.

One day he tried to escape. And miraculously, he succeeded. During the wildest of desert storms when visibility was almost zero, he slipped through a damaged fence. He sped off hidden by the storm and travelled freely for some time. They hunted him with dogs and four-wheel drive vehicles but the weather, which was wild, covered his tracks.

When the tempest at last abated, freedom seemed to be his. But he stumbled across one of the dogs which had in the confusion, been struck and severely injured by a pursuit vehicle.

The Shepherd lay still and apparently dead in the dust at his feet. Then it quivered. It was stretched out, wounded and in pain on the track hovering around death.

M1359 bent down and touched the suffering creature's elegant, grey neck. It turned its head, looked at him with its dark, suffering eyes and breathed a soft cry of pain.

That chance pathos left the fugitive no choice. The experiences of his own life bound him in a strange way to the creature. He could not leave him there.

Gently, almost lovingly, he took the animal in his arms, turned and came back to this place. After a long walk, he stood before the cold, impenetrable gates, holding the dog in his arms, waiting for the guards to let him in. Where else could he have gone?

And so his mandatory detention became a coalition of the willing. The dog survived.

Here he was forced to stay once more, incarcerated for a whole year. And then another until years lost their significance. A touch of compassion, from somewhere in the administration, gave him time exercising the institution's dogs around the inner perimeter of the centre.

These times gave him moments of happiness. One of the dogs was always glad to see him.

On the third day of this week just passed, my dear child, this man who had befriended me, was found dead in his cell. No one has told me how he died.

M1359 has at last gone forever from this place.

With love,

Narni.

* * * * *

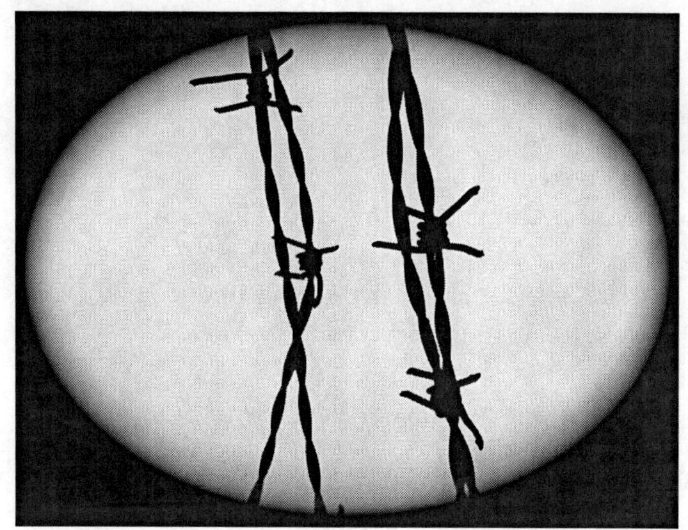
Stay!

III

Icarus

**A robin redbreast in a cage
Puts all Heaven in a rage.**

— William Blake

Dearest Laura,
Who Lived Once
Where All Things Are Loved And Free,

O there is still pain of my aching limbs! How I long to walk freely in the open countryside!

Thoughts are a problem here, dear child. There is such a weight of evidence against the validity of this place. To make people lonely without listening to their stories is surely a crime.

To live alone day after day destroys your serenity faster than disease can destroy your body. It can be a tormenting thing and angry thoughts have no trouble seizing you because there is nobody else to protect you. Invented demons stalk you here and will not leave you alone, even though your imagination reaches out for peace and tries to find you a friend. Any friend will do.

There are all kinds of prisons Laura. But unjust isolation is the deepest, darkest dungeon of them all.

That is why, here in this place, I constantly long for more company. Here at night I am truly alone in a tiny room although there are always people around me, some in uniforms and others clothed in sameness.

In the daytime they speak to me occasionally. But mostly in recent times, their voices seem light years away. Sometimes only the stars can hear my replies.

Yet in spite of this, memories often comfort me. That is where I find you again. And my parents of so long ago. And the creatures of my distant, early happiness.

I see that butterfly with the red and black wings, which danced on that flower in my childhood garden. I see that tree which seemed to know me and held me in its arms when I dared to climb it.

And there, I can see them: the cricket which I startled one day into flight, the spider which always seemed to spin its delicate lace in the morning, and my childhood friend the cat which played with that ball of wool as if the ball were alive.

They still live, as beautiful as ever, in the museum of my thoughts.

Some time ago, my dearest child, one of the truest friends I have ever found suddenly entered this dejected life of mine without the permission of my captors. He has no number here, because he is a bird.

It was an almost fatal day for him. He flew into the ledge of the only window of my cell and fell through it at my feet. He was stunned and at first, seemed to be dead.

I gently picked him up and found a soft place for him. I spoke soothingly to my poor visitor. You should always speak to birds with your kindest voice because they understand more than you know.

'Poor Icarus,' I said. 'Don't despair. You will recover.' I was delighted to see him come to life after some time. He stretched hesitantly and seemed to see me through one anguished eye.

Soon, although terribly wracked by pain and barely able to move, he was glad to sip some of my water and in a little while to nibble some of my bread. That was how our friendship began. He was content to stay with me, for he was hurt and not fit to travel.

The guards saw him and did not seem to mind. Soon he began to take some of my crumbs from my own hand. We talked to each other and in some strange way, for a brief time, we shared a surprising happiness.

Time flew, even though my bird could not. After a few days, my partner Icky began to move more freely. He stretched his wings and obviously began once more to feel like a bird. But he stayed with me.

Then one day I noticed what seemed to be a twinkle in his eye. Perhaps it was time to set him free.

So I walked to the door leading to the cramped courtyard outside my cell. He followed me as a groundling. Then I opened the door.

There was a sudden flutter of excitement. And then a hop and a skip. A dark grey feathery flash hurtled past me up, up into the sky. Above the walls, above the brutality of wire and it seemed to be flying beyond the eternal imprisonment of time.

As I watched, I somehow felt I too was set free. I became very lonely again in my little room for a while. I missed those eyes, which watched my every move. And the joy of another creature caring about my existence. But slowly I learned to accept my fate.

Some more days slid reluctantly by. These days became weeks. The weeks became months. Icarus had flown into my past. Loneliness tiptoed behind me, taunting me in the hollowness of each day until a whole year had passed. That was when events mysteriously reshaped themselves.

All was still in the emptiness of my room. My eyes had become dimmed once more, by the repetitive consistency of things. Those glazed windows of my mind had stopped noticing little changes. They did not see at first, what my ears had suddenly noticed. It was a cheery, musical call.

There on the sill he was once more: Icky. My heavenly messenger fluttered his angel feathers of friendship. He cocked his head in happy greeting and once again celebrated by taking simple morsels from my hand. My feathered companion had returned.

How can I tell you how happy this made me? What is happiness if it is not the light in a true friend's eyes?

And so my dearest Laura, the one person I always long to see, you can understand that I have now another friend to visit me. He comes and goes in his own time and at his own chosen speed. But always he comes back

Today was again a time to leave. I said goodbye once more to my bird. When he flew away, he seemed to take some of my despair with him.

'Icarus', I said, 'Wait for me next time you leave. I might be ready to fly with you.'

He left me feeling less alone.

Icarus has not gone forever from this place. But some birds, like some men, will never be caged.

Rest well, dear nestling.

Narni.

* * * * *

I missed those eyes, which watched my every move.

IV

The Velvet Mask

Where drums beat, laws are silent.

— Cicero

Dearest Laura,
Child of Tranquility,

More bullying today. Three big men demanded my secrets. I said, 'If I tell them to you, they will not be secrets.' They punished me for that.

So I escaped into my imagination. O the mind, mind has canyons. Today I began to think I might be insane. Madness is a powerful enemy when it recruits you into its presence.

I am haunted by dark delusions. I know there is another prison on another island, far across the world, where freedom and justice are even more relentlessly kept outside the walls. I know it is far away, that nightmare without a night. Yet somehow, I have begun to see it as part of this place too. The problem with my insanity is I have come to believe that other Hell is here.

I keep imagining one special location within this internment centre where madness is king and torture is a liveried servant. It is a separate and isolated section. Just down the hallway. A secret place made valid by allegedly exceptional circumstances. A special category: Preventive Detention. There control can last, if the gaolers choose, beyond forever.

This savagery is endlessly described to me by my inner voices. Crazy! Crazy! Crazy!

It is nearby. I can feel it.

Prisoners have no identity there. They are alien ideas not people. They walk only if chained to guards. The space they are in never changes. And they are never seen by outsiders.

Hail 1679, the Holy Year! But Habeas Corpus in this black hole within my mind is an effigy burnt at a stake.

The place I speak of cannot be here. Not here! Not here! It must be somewhere else.

I know this, yet I keep hearing tales floating on the air, which say the opposite. The voices keep talking to me, telling me the stories of the people who are forced to live in that closed space.

Time is naked there, the voices say. There are no hours or days, only extensions of pain. All patterns of time are reduced to a straight line . . . the shortest distance between two infinities.

And as for the guards. Their prisoners are flies to wanton boys. The eyes of justice do not see what happens there. All things are permitted because there is no scrutiny. No redress.

In my delusion the voices whispered to me recently that into this endless persecution was thrust an exceptional man. Not an ordinary character whose fate is decided by carefully compiled charges. Not a benign, conforming creature who answers the beck and call of obsessive masters. But a dangerous suspect. A pre-selected enemy whose face, by the decree of authority, must be hidden behind a velvet mask. He is verdict without a trial.

The voices come to me at night in this place and tell me things about this man. The voices whisper. One should always listen to the whispers.

This unique person, the voices tell me, was or is so dangerous that he could not be seen in public and, even though he lives in darkness, he is forced forever to wear the velvet mask.

From the first, he was considered of such deadly potential that he was branded never to be released, and required to remain eternally masked and in silence. None but a tiny cabal know he is there. A yet smaller clique know who he is.

Why you may ask? What could he possibly have done to earn such punishment? War crimes? Treason? Betrayal of people in power? A threat of betrayal?

The voices tell me, in this place, there is no obligation to explain. He is simply a useful symbol of danger. A catalyst for conflict derived from fear. No explanation is required. Only his eternal silence.

And what of the nature and length of his punishment? Are there degrees of menace deserving of such contempt? To be forbidden to give your name or even to speak to another person on pain of instant death?

You might question the feasibility of such a murder of freedom in the modern, civilized world. But remember. Remember--on Devil's Islands, such things are possible.

My dear child, all men are fugitives in one way or another. I see figures in velvet masks everywhere: whistle-blowers; pacifists; insurgents; Dreamtime dwellers; queers.

In the past, Dietrich Bonhoeffer wore such a mask, as did Bartolomeo Vanzetti and Nicolo Sacco and Julius and Ethel Rosenberg. How can we know who else is masked in velvet when Habeas Corpus is dead and there is no separation of the powers?

Ah! this poor, benighted man. I keep hearing about him, locked in his torture. He notices only his enemies around him. Many are unseen. People of his past. The guards of his present. And people he is yet to meet. Always plotting to keep him under their control. Fear my child, is a learned experience.

Absolute power allows no escape. If you are a threat to ambitious men, the danger will follow you wherever you may run. That is why we good people must be prepared for any sacrifice to protect from abuse the child we call Truth.

Anxiety never lets me go. It haunts my nights. Voices harangue me, telling me that to be silent is to consent. I must talk about him lest one day the owners of different voices may come knocking on my door in the middle of the night and take me away.

Alas my loved one, in this fiery world the reputations of other people are deadly dangerous. Because of what you say or do or think, they can be arrows pointed at your heart.

You and I and all others are vulnerable to punishment for things we know. Things we have done. Things we should have done. Things we are going to do. Or even things we would never do.

This man in my dream has no number. He stays a prisoner of my mind. Yet somewhere in the real world you will find his brothers. His demons will patently lie in wait there, for them. His brothers too will never be free.

Creeping tangible monsters tangled in their awareness. Things in a cell to bite you, and infect you with their venom. Things which crawl up your body. They are all their demons.

Nanoscale intruders for your eyes only, pin pricks watching you in this darkened box of a cell and keeping you under their spell.

Not a box but a tin. Not a tin but a bag. Not a bag but a shell. Not a shell but a cage. Not a cage but a coffin. It is merely a container of living flesh. O why hast thou forsaken me?

And the night controllers. There they will be again at the end of every day . . . wherever you look. Being confined, you alone will see them . . . hormone-filled spiders waiting for lights-out, to patter like horses on pavements out of their hiding places and stare at you unseen, with never-blinking eyes, lusting for a chance to spring and sink their fangs into the back of your neck.

You hear their footsteps coming towards you? Here they come. Here they come. They are coming now. Now, not later. Now. Now.

They own the darkness. They tell it what to do. They cry out in your face while others hear nothing. Their clip clop clip clop coming towards you will not stop! And the voices. Chattering secretly with the wind. Talking about you and other people. Hatching plots against you with such cunning that only you can know of them. Only you can hear them.

And the drums that go with them. Strange echoes of your heart. Growing louder with your own excitement. Railing to a rallentando as eventually you writhe into the oblivion of unending wakefulness.

The drums in fact can never cease. No relief. No respite from torture. No peace. All these things. It would be better to be a beast turned into meat on broken bones. That would give you peace.

No escape from this madness. Nowhere to turn. No escape until the future dies and you decide that the drums have to end. Until you decide to take off your velvet mask.

That is what you do. You take off your velvet mask and kill yourself by revealing your name. Suicide is your only escape.

Then almost instantly, masked prisoner, you are dead.

They bury you then, like that ancient prisoner in the old Bastille, under a false name. Out in the desert where wild flowers grow on your grave.

Oh no no no no no no no no no no no no no! This cannot be true. This suffering imposed by man on man could not be part of the real world.

Laura. Please forgive these recent cries of mine. I know you will be patient and understand the tempests of my torment.

In spite of all this, my dear child, never discount the potency of compassion. It can bring such a man as this, masked and unnumbered, into the shelter of your company. What if he exists only in our minds?

Where else can you find truth but in your mind?

When freedom is crushed by preventive detention, this masked person could be imprisoned anywhere. Even in a room next door. He could be me. Or you.

Then we would see, in full colour, exactly what he sees. Things only victims can see. And if we are not careful, some day the drums of his pounding heart may beat in time with our own.

It may be wise to take no further notice of this letter, dearest one. See it as the discourse of a haunted mind. But nevertheless, be kind to any troubled soul you meet.

Good night fragrant child. I must end my fantasy now.

Let the man in the velvet mask be gone forever from this place.

Narni

* * * * *

This man in my dream has no number. He stays a prisoner of my mind. Yet somewhere in the real world you will find his brothers. His demons will patently lie in wait there for them. His brothers too will never be free.

V

Mots Sans Frontières

There was an owl liv'd in an oak,
The more he heard the less he spoke;
The less he spoke, the more he heard,
O, if men were all like that wise bird.

— Punch, Vol. 68, 155, 1875

Dearest Laura,
Who Still Speaks To Me,

Violence came back today. They crushed me more energetically this morning. They pushed me and I fell. They were very angry with me for some reason. They shouted at me and threw daggers with their eyes, which whistled past my ears.

After solitary for seven days, they seemed to think I would confess. But I had nothing to confess. They must have been on a false trail. Now I am back in my cell. Peace has broken out.

Normal routine at last has returned. Now I have time to think of you again, my dear child. As a result of all this, my love for you has grown even stronger. I must tell you another story. This time a happier one.

*****

Freedom, liberty, independence, breathing space, truth; they are no more than words here. Nothing more.

Words, Laura, can be friends or violent missiles. They can start wars or they can inspire peace. In spite of their serious functions, words can also colour your life with laughter. Do you remember how we giggled at funny names when you were a little girl?

This morning I found again among my scraps of paper a letter from another prisoner of this place, M1001. He was an inmate from not long ago who struggled with English words.

That letter gave me a reason to laugh again, in spite of my recent pain. I must tell you this story.

One poet said, dear Laura, that words are loaded pistols. To some people they are much more.

They are dangerous cannons. We can become terribly afraid of them. It is so easy to fear what you do not understand. And it is such a lonely struggle if the words you are looking for belong in foreign mouths.

There are 7,000 different languages in the world. Today, only half of them are being taught to children; which means that in a lifetime half of the world's language pool will disappear. With these losses will go history, poetry, theatre, and wisdom in various other forms. So Laura, we must share our words.

There came a time when M1001 became very busy, because of an approaching interview which was for citizenship in this land. His desperate wish was to speak well and to understand, so that he could deserve to belong to this country. I will explain his struggle.

It was some moons ago when M1001 begged me to help him learn more about words. One day he gave me this letter telling me about some of his troubles. This is how the letter begins.

> Dear Friend
> My language is in hospital. He is very sick. I am sad because I try very hard with English but she still tricks me. It keeps changing it's mind. Can you please talk to me about the problems I write out for you. It is very important to me. Here is my list of troubles . . .

Poor M1001. He had so many problems with the English language that his list was very long.

I read it carefully. Then, when next we met, we talked and I began to do my best to help him. It is fun to be a teacher.

'O brother! You are very kind to help me,' he said, as we stood unobtrusively together, talking. 'These are big problems.'

'Soon I do Citizenship Test and have interview. I learn many answers because I love this country. But I cannot work out de questions to put with de answers.'

'Don't worry, my friend,' I said. 'Do not be afraid of examinations. Any fool can ask a wise man questions he cannot answer. That way they discover only what the wise man doesn't know and never have the benefit of the wise man's wisdom.'

'But come on,' I went on in my most encouraging voice. 'Let us simply have some fun. Fun with words.

'OK,' he replied. 'Let us start.

What is a fuckwit? Can you please help me to be one so I can be popular and famous like the Prime Minister the cleaner talked about?'

'Not a good idea,' I replied and explained to him why. He gurgled in the back of his throat with amused surprise.

'Aha! Thank you. Now I know. Thank you. Thank you very much.'

After a pause, he said, 'Now what is this rest bite after hard work?'

'It is not a rest bite. It is a respite, which means 'a rest'; what everyone needs after hard work. That is the way they talk here.'

'Thank you,' he nodded with a smile.

Then with a serious expression, 'Why in this land are animals allowed to vote?'

'They are not.'

'Yes they are. I am reading about a man in parliament who capture the donkey vote.'

'Aha! That is a joke. It is about people who mark voting sheets from top to bottom without thinking. They are 'donkeys' or stupid animals.

We both laughed, but only for a little while. He was anxious to continue.

'All right then. Can you tell me who is Johnny Bliss? He seems to be in the toilets often because Charlie, the only friendly cleaner I know, keeps going there for him.'

Now I laughed. 'No my friend, it is a rhyme with 'piss'. That is a way they say things here. It's a joke.'

M1001's eyes opened wide. The light of awareness came to his face.

He gave a surprised nod and smiled a little.

'Then who is Edgar Britts? The guard with the big black belt says I give him to him.'

'More rhyme,' I said, 'It really means 'shits'.

A sad look. 'Thank you my friend. I see. I see.'

Now a pause.

'Then can you tell me why my cousin Rico who come by aeroplane is called "Immigrant" while I who come by boat is called "boat-person"? Are we not both same species?'

Another pause.

'That is one thing I cannot help you with my friend. It is something to do with money and trust. Bad names are handy when you wish to gain power and win arguments. Many people have been made afraid of boatpeople. But many are not.'

'Uh huh. OK. Then why cannot the Immigration Minister find a grand piano in a one-roomed house? Big puzzle.'

'That one is easy,' I laughed. 'It's another joke by someone who doesn't like him. It means he is too stupid to see simple things. He couldn't find the nose on his own face.'

'Ha! Aha!' M1001 guffawed with me in his gentle, humble, well-meaning way. 'You little ripper mate! I get it!'

'Why do we hear about free gifts? Are not all gifts free?'

'Yes.'

'And what about this one? Why do they make people in this country who are running late drag chains everywhere? Is that a punishment? Big worry to me. Very mean trick on poor late person. Will they do that to me as punishment? I not surprised if they do.'

'No reason to worry, my dear friend. It's another way they speak here. If you have to drag something, it makes you slower. And that makes you late. When you are late you only seem to be dragging a chain. It's not a punishment. It is what we call a metaphor. A metaphor pretends one thing is something else to help us understand.'

'Ah! I see. Thank you my good friend. Metaphor. I think I see. Metaphor. Metaphor.'

'But there is something else I do not understand. If 'insane' mean not sane, 'insincere' mean not sincere and 'invisible' mean not visible, why do inflammable things burn?'

'I see your problem my friend. It's big. But with this, I can help you.

'You see words are not like people. They have been welcomed into English for thousands of years from every place on earth. Now in their English they use words from everywhere. You and I and all others from different countries in our world have different ways of saying things.

'Inflammable' and 'insane' come from different places, so they do not have to mean the same things. 'Insane' comes from Italy where 'insane' always meant 'not sane'. 'Inflammable' comes from France where it first meant 'can burn'.

'Do not worry too much my friend. It is hard for everyone. Even the Australians who make fun of foreigners' funny mistakes, do not understand all the words they use.

'Words need you to love them. If you are patient and learn to understand them, they become your very best friends.'

M1001 took both of my hands. He nodded. There was a light in his eyes.

For many more days we talked on about words throughout the exercise period. We were happy together.

He had countless other problems. He was a good learner who dearly wished to learn.

'What is a dunny? And why is its glass door useless?'

'Is Emma Chisit a woman? '

'Who is Larry and why is he happy?'

'Why does Hughie send us rain when we ask him?'

'Why do Australians use banjos as frying pans, shovels and shoulders of mutton?'

'Why is a farmer in a truck a ball-bearing cowboy?

It all very . . . How you say it? . . . tricky.'

'Why is a bastard lucky? And if he is, why did they run over him long time ago?'

'Why are kind bankers as scarce as rocking horse manure?'

'Why did that guard tell me, "If it was raining pea soup I'd get hit on the head with a fork"?'

'Why is a policeman called a bluebottle?'

Ah Laura, I had such fun sharing ideas with M1001 and trying to explain! He worked so hard. He wanted so much to belong to this culture that he became obsessed with the learning.

I told him that there is a way over every mountain. He smiled. 'Thank you my friend,' he finally said. 'You give me the good word and make my mountain small.'

Words, dear Laura, are not afterthoughts tacked onto existence. They are life itself. We cannot live without them.

And as for metaphors; they are the fabric of our society. They are the houses in which we live. They are all we have when new ideas run faster than our pens.

We even talked of punctuation.

'Are not words more important than dots and dashes?' he said.

'Ah, my friend,' I replied. 'Punctuation can change everything. It is the signpost of meaning. Look. I will show you.'

I wrote for him this sentence: *A woman without her man is nothing.*

'True,' he said. 'I agree with that.'

'Not necessarily so,' I replied. 'Some women will disagree. Watch me make the same words mean something completely different.'

Then I wrote: *A woman; without her, man is nothing.*

We both laughed. He understood.

'Or look at this,' I continued and wrote for him: *Private. No swimming allowed.* I changed it to this: *Private? No. Swimming allowed.*

We both laughed some more. He understood.

All of our efforts seem to have worked. Perhaps his talks with me have made him a new citizen for them. Perhaps unlike many others, he has passed their test.

I am sure words are one of the reasons he has left us a long time ago.

M1001 has gone now forever from this place.

Narni.

* * * * *

VI

Oscar

Mutato nomine de te fabula narratur.
With the name changed, the story applies to you.
— Horace

Dearest Laura,
Lover of Bright Colours,

Another story. I find out things but do not always understand why. I listen to real cries at times from different cells nearby. I believe I am not the only one punished with suffering in this place.

* * * * *

I have shared my life here for a brief time with another: with M1717. He told me of how he gave himself a new name, Ongo Bongo Letimavit, before he left The United States of America. That name is unknown in this establishment.

He is black. He is torn and worn and weary. And his face is famous. Not so with either of his names.

You see, in the late 1940s he was a young film actor. His roles were not of heroes but black undesirables. He always played the part of a savage. A menacing, murderous person. A terrifying extra.

He had to act to earn money for food and life for his family. To keep his job he was forced to fuel the fires of prejudice against colour and difference by being dangerous and black in countless movies.

Where the white adventurer needed someone to kill, he was there. When the white hunter needed a new menace to destroy, he was there. When the beautiful white girl needed the direst of dangers, he was there. There was plenty of work for him, and all he needed to be was the subservient shadow of his true self, mumbling a few invented words and pulling ugly or fearsome faces. But truth fled.

There were never long lines to learn. Never challenging moments of thoughtful dignity. The only requirements were gestures of menace and anger, spears, a black skin and an improvised guttural pretence of language.

As the years passed, this good and loving man grew tired of being hazardous and evil. He longed to play the role of a kind and positive human! How he longed to bring to a role the gathered wisdom of his life and share it with people of every colour!

But it was not to be. His wife had died two years before. His two children had grown to be preoccupied with their own affairs. There was nothing left to him but celluloid pretentiousness.

Time went by. Eventually, age began to reduce the aura and menace of his presence. He could feel the end approaching. One black day, he reached a crisis point probably linked to his steadily evolving despair.

It had been a long morning. The heat of the lights on the set was more oppressive than usual. My friend had just missed a cue and was wounded by the sharp tongues of both the director and the white actor.

During the retake, something snapped and he lost the place. Instead of running away in fear from the fictitious hero as the script required, he turned and faced him, throwing away his spear.

Then M1717 directed the irresistible force of his fist to the centre of the white actor's face. The white man dropped far more quickly than the countless villains he himself had slain in earlier movies. M1717 stepped over the prostrate form with the cameras still rolling. He turned and faced the lenses.

'Good and evil have no colour,' he cried. Then he turned his back on everything and left the scene forever.

That was how he became a hobo. As one final gesture of defiant protest he changed his name by deed poll to Ongo Bongo Letimavit. The given names stood for his meaningless film-speak. The family name was to remind him of the last thing he did on camera.

A bleak year passed. A year of stolen warmth from footpath grates and scavenged, discarded food.

Then final despair set in like winter rain. Complete poverty. No money means no hope in that world, whatever the other circumstances which befall. He decided to flee overseas by the only means possible, as a stowaway on a very old merchant ship.

Despite his poverty he was still strong. Still an optimist.

He dreamed of Africa and a new life of happiness. There, in a new dream, he would stand free on an African mountain and sing songs of his own choice with his own rich, deep voice. He was ready to fight for happiness.

He would act again, and write, and make films of a different kind. Perhaps he would discover a companion for his twilight years.

But what a journey it was instead! Constant motion of dying ship against angry waves. Fumes and darkness. Groaning, shaking, struggling engines. He became very ill amidst the rats and filth below decks.

Eventually he had no choice but to reveal who he was and beg for help. As a consequence, he was put ashore in this country.

Eventually he came to this place. His crime: to be black, poor, without papers and to have travelled by sea. He stayed here for many months while various negotiations took place.

His dreams dissolved into emptiness. But even so, he talked to me. We talked in the exercise yard of more important things than cabbages and kings.

We journeyed in our minds past the dangers and heroic rescues of his Hollywood films to a higher plane. He was such an interesting companion, in spite of the white muzzles, which had silenced him for so long.

And then, with no advanced notice, he was deported to America. He was whisked away. One day here and the next gone.

He gave me just a fleeting notice of his departure and handed me the battered book he had carried with him forever. It was a copy of *A Tale of Two Cities*. He had written on the front page: 'Never the best, only the worst.'

A new face now peers out from his cell.

My dear Laura, I knew M1717 would continue his search for compassion and understanding, wherever he was taken. Later, purely by chance, I discovered that there has been a happy ending to this story.

It was an amazing turn of fortune. It made me think there may be hope for all of us. This battered, kind and clever man has succeeded beyond even my dreams. Merit does charm the soul--eventually.

In an old newspaper lying on the laundry floor I read that M1717, our movie-house ghost, had at last come back to life as a writer in the United States. My fellow internee, whose former existence once made him unknown and unwanted in an indifferent world, has grown through adversity and discovered his voice.

Now, suddenly he has found a friend called Oscar. He has won an Academy Award for Best Screenplay with the film *Black Is The Colour Of My True Love's Hair*. All he needed was the escape from here ironically provided by his keepers.

Totus mundis agit histrionem: 'All the world loves to bring a story to life.' The message above the door of Shakespeare's *Globe*, has evolved into 'All the world's a stage.' Some tales may be full of sound and fury, but few signify nothing.

My child you can see that the Elizabethans knew that stories are guardians of the future. The story of tomorrow depends on where the plots of today lead us.

Sleep well dear rose. Flowers can grow in many gardens.

M1717 has gone now forever from this place.

Narni.

* * * * *

Where the white adventurer needed someone to kill, he was there. When the white hunter needed a new menace to destroy, he was there. When the beautiful white girl needed the direst of dangers, he was there. There was plenty of work for him, and all he needed to be was the subservient shadow of his true self, mumbling a few invented words and pulling ugly or fearsome faces. But truth fled.

VII

A Little Terror

Hunger is the best sauce.

— Cicero

Dearest Laura,
Child of the All-seeing Stars,

Some more bullying again today, but I am learning to smile to ease the pain. One of them, a gentler bully, stopped the other from hitting me.

When I think of you I think of a flower, Clianthus, which means in ancient Greek 'glory flower'. There is one in this species called Sturt's Desert Pea, in the bush outside my prison. It is black and crimson and heroic. I think of it often. It gives me strength. I know it is nearby. Somewhere.

I have been thinking too that memories are precious. Sometimes they are all we have.

Do you remember our rice puddings? Our apricots? Our magic bottle of sweets? They remind me of another story.

* * * * *

Another man I found here, M1231, had his own special taste delight, which he dearly missed. In this regimented place with its boring fare, he was desperate to savour his favourite food: bologna.

'Ah!' he would say, 'If only I could once more taste bologna. Then I would be happy to rot away in this house of devils.'

A famous English writer once taught us that taste and smell are the parents of memory. It was true for this fellow prisoner of mine, Laura. His longing for his past, his wish to recall the little village in the hills of his home was undoubtedly linked to the experience of eating bologna.

Perhaps this is why his craving became an obsession. He wrote letters in Italian to the Prime Minister demanding appropriate food to reduce some of the suffering of this place. To the Immigration Minister. To the Premier of the state. And to the Queen. All in vain.

Nobody bothered to read them. In fact they were not even posted but thrown into the camp incinerator. So he went on a hunger strike.

'I rather die than be any longer without my bologna,' he said. 'More important than life.' But that failed too when he was force-fed.

Now, there is a place which is very run down but important to some people, about sixty miles from this detention centre, across the desert. It is a tumble-down pub called 'The Last Post'.

One of the guards, on his way home on leave, apparently called in there for food and drink. It seems he had heard of M1231's plight and shared his story with mine host. It just happened that in that hotel, working as a cook, was an ancient Italian they lovingly called Rigoletto. He too overheard the guard's tale.

I am sure Italians have proved themselves in history to be very compassionate people. Rigoletto certainly was. He was also a master cook.

Although he was a tough old man who despised much of the world and many of the people he found around him, there was more than one serve of kindness in his heart. He could not bear the thought of a compatriot deprived of his favourite Italian food.

So he decided to do something about it. He set about creating an exquisite sample of the meat to bring to the internment-centre.

The choicest pork. The tenderest beef. A touch of bacon. A sprinkle of rabbit. Even a dabble of kangaroo. And an array of heavenly spices, all found their way into the sausage.

Then, driving his old horse and cart on a whole afternoon's journey, the old man came with the meat to the prison camp. The journey took so long that when it ended, the world was almost in darkness. The sun had just set, gates were fast, and the establishment was locked up for the night.

Undeterred, Rigoletto dismounted from his bedraggled cart and began to call M1231's name in a loud and echoing voice.

'Gi-o-van-ni! Gi-o-van-ni! Gi-o-van-ni'!

'Bologna! Bologna! Bologna! Bologna!

Gi-o-van-ni bologna! Bologna! Bologna! Giovanni bologna!'

At the time, M1231 happened to be sitting on the toilet in the washroom section of one wing of the centre. He could not believe the words he was hearing. With a rapid restoration of decorum, he leapt from the toilet block and ran towards the sound of the compassionate visiting angel.

'Cannot come in. I am going home. It is far. I must go now. Can you catch the sausage?'

'Yes! I catch it. Throw it. Throw it. Throw it.'

So with a deep breath and careful aim, Rigoletto hurled the sausage over the wire walls, across the exercise area towards M1231. It swirled and twirled and whirled through the evening light.

Now Chance can be a devilish thing if it has a mind to be. At that very moment, one of the lookouts in the watchtower heard the shouting and happened to turn to see the throw and then the sausage flying through the air.

Unfortunately, a guard on observation duty in such half-light cannot tell the difference between a sausage and a terrorist's bomb. The sentries in this place have been rigorously conditioned to be instantly ready for danger.

As a consequence, this one feared the worst and reacted with the required lightning speed. He pressed a button. Sirens and alarm bells began to ring. Security staff and their dogs almost instantly appeared out of the gathering darkness.

Routine is law, rather than reasoning, at such times so the alarm and fracas triggered a further chain reaction. Every servant of the centre responded to a red alert.

And things got worse. Spontaneous alarums were transmitted to the appropriate government departments far across the desert. Air bases were given a code red. A helicopter was immediately scrambled. It contained a small SWAT team, which arrived soon after the sausage had landed.

Sadly for M1231, that heaven-sent sausage fell tauntingly just out of his reach. Undaunted, he painfully stretched his arm through the wires. Inch by inch. It was so close he could almost smell the delicious meat.

His fingers stretched towards it. So near. He knew he could reach it. His arm grew longer. And longer. His fingertips touched the skin of the sausage.

At that very instant one of the passing guard-dogs snatched it away from him in an ecstasy of delight. A sharp word from its handler split the night air and the dog immediately dropped its treasure.

A robot detection device quickly appeared. It waddled purposefully towards the apparent missile.

That inspection did not take long. There was an order. Then a shout of all clear. And then, to the dog's obvious joy, the 'missile' returned to the dog's jaws.

M1231 cried.

Explanations followed. There was a high-powered, routine enquiry. One or two heads fell and changes were made. Future checks and balances were established.

I am also glad to tell you my Sicilian fellow-prisoner, after a day or so, was given peace. A very large piece of bologna. Rigoletto kindly came back--with another sausage. This time, it reached its mark.

Dearest Laura. One man's meat is another man's poison.

Repercussions continued. The incident seems to have set other wheels in motion. I noticed just three weeks later that another cell was empty.

M1231 had been deported to Italy. Exactly why, I do not know. But there is nothing strange about such changes in this place. People go without fanfare.

And so the story ended. I love telling you these tales Laura. You might say that I collect other men's flowers here, and provide nothing but my own words as the string to tie them together.

And M1231 has gone now forever from this place. Perhaps he has eventually returned to Bologna.

Narni.

* * * * *

VIII

A Kind of Dreaming

Amor vincit omnia et nos cedamus amori
Love conquers all and let us yield to it

— Virgil

Dearest Laura,
Who Lives Beyond Sorrow,

The physical torture of this place is still taunting me. My limbs are aching more today. But age is no doubt a reason too, so I will not complain.

Hatreds, kidnapping, disappearances, outsourced torture, cruel and inhuman treatment, unwanted war: they are all behind or related to the walls of the new brand of asylum refuges.

Dear child of mine. How is your life progressing as you read this? Are you growing weary of my words? I thank you for sharing my life here through my letters. But you have shared so much of my life already. Do you remember when I read you the tale of *Monkey* and he taught us not to love for return but to forgive endlessly?

M1611 was yet another vulnerable man who passed by me here.

His life was crushed under the wheels of fortune. He fled from Iraq by sea. His genes were among the pitiful few left of a race with a recorded history of at least five thousand years.

There were no personal papers when he came to this land. No verifiable identity. In this arena, he was a body with no right to exist. He was a vacuum without a name. Nothing but a number.

You, my treasured child, walking as you do through the dauntless days of youth, cannot imagine the depth of the shadows in his eyes when he spoke to me of his loss. He was a Mandaean. The word *manda*, which identifies his crushed people, means 'knowledge' in his language. But where has all the knowledge gone, long time passing?

We talked about life for many hours. Although we both had common words to share, I mourned with him the approaching demise of his native language.

To pass the time and lighten our days, M1611 and I pretended to be poets. We wrote verse and shared it aloud when next we met. We playfully challenged each other from time to time with rhyme.

'This day must mend, but will not end,' he said to me one day. My response was, 'No end is in sight till day turns to night.' Whereupon he replied smilingly, thinking he would out-rhyme me, 'No gratitude lives in this latitude.' I gave an impromptu reply to his challenge: 'Perhaps, since a dirty rat it chewed.'

We both laughed. The hues of sunsets for many days revived our memories. We were glad to have each other to talk to. We spoke of countless things and wandered together among the histories of our different people. We even shared our dreams.

On one these days, we wrote this poem together. The ideas belonged to both of us.

Quietus

We are not dismayed in this tortured place
When we feel the breath of hate upon our face.
Instead we dream of a future curtain call
And a merciful wind which blows upon us all.

For we have learnt that in death each prison Devil
Will die and decay with us at the very same level.
So that is why we are given to present laughter
As we wait with joy for the justice of the hereafter.

I shared with him the struggle with words for a long time. Thinking and nodding. Struggling and still nodding. He did not lose his smile. Laughter is a cure for many things.

The words of this poem cajoled a smile onto the lips of my friend. For about a year, I observed M1611 bravely endure the sadness of the ongoing, changeless days. We joked and laughed as often as we could. Until a dramatic change altered both our lives.

He fell suddenly very ill. Terribly ill. His head ached mercilessly. His eyesight began to play strange tricks and then to fail. Movement became agony.

Death was seen by the prison authority to be lurking. He was therefore taken into the intensive care of the Good Companion Hospital, a long way from this place. It is a small but well-equipped medical sanctuary.

Glioblastoma Grade IV was the illness. Cancer needs no visa.

The surgery was urgent. The resources of this lucky country, previously unavailable, were now marshalled in the presence of death to treat the unwanted visitor to its shores. He was well and professionally cared for. There was constant watch over him in his grave condition.

M1611 survived the operation. At the moment of recovery he opened his eyes and looked into the face of a nurse who was anxiously watching him. He was heavily sedated as consciousness returned. For him it had become a strangely distorted world.

He had very little voice and what was left seemed reluctant to leave his mouth.

'Is . . . is this Heaven?' he asked the nurse on duty softly in faltering English.

The nurse smiled. She touched his shoulder reassuringly. She was obviously pleased with his return to consciousness.

'No,' she said. 'Not unless you decide it is.'

M1611 closed his eyes and fell back into sleep. When he awoke some hours later, the same nurse had returned and was busily adjusting the bed and the curtain and the drip above his head.

'What is name?' he said.

'Mirinda,' she replied without stopping her work. She did not tell him that Mirinda is an Aboriginal word which means 'beautiful woman'. M1611 looked through his pain at the black curls of her hair and admired her thin, lithe body as she worked.

'Names are not really necessary among busy friends,' she said softly. 'Rest well now and we'll soon have you out of here.'

He noticed her flashing white teeth and her deep, dark eyes.

'What if I not want to leave? If I leave I go back to Hell not Heaven?'

She smiled sadly and did not reply as she busily wrote on his chart. Then she briefly raised her eyes and looked at him as he seemed once more asleep.

He spoke, catching her by surprise.

'Will you marry me?'

She laughed, slightly embarrassed, and did not reply.

'I have no family left in world. No friends in this country. Eventually these people here send me back to my land where war and death is. But would be big pity. I can be good man in this country.'

She listened despite her preoccupation but still did not reply. He was silent for a few faltering minutes with his eyes closed. Then he spoke, almost awake again.

'I speak Aramaic and Persian well. I improve my English. I write poems. Have degree from Padua. I not much speak English but I know my country's story and other things well.'

'And I love you.'

This time she laughed aloud. 'You can't LOVE me. We have only spoken to each other for about ten minutes.'

'O yes I do. I love you gentle hand that touch me and work hard for me. I love you kind eyes that see me and not look past me. I love you white smile, which give me sunshine.

'Will you marry me?'

'Time for rest,' she said.

'Will you marry me?'

The nurse gave a gentle but friendly laugh. She was used to patients' odd behaviour. 'I'll think about it. But rest now.'

He knew her aim was to stop him from talking. Finally, he lapsed again into sedation. She left him to his sleep and dreams of courtship.

Brain tumours give no quarter and pay no attention to race or political status. Their cause is unknown, so despair cannot be discounted as a possibility.

M1611 had less than three months to live. He was humanely given shelter in a public cancer ward. After a week in intensive care, he was moved to another section of the hospital where life was more apparent. The windows opened onto trees in the hospital grounds and revealed the cloudy sky-world in the distance across the red plains.

M1611 could hear birds in the trees. They were free he thought. The wind ruffled the leaves to the bird music.

Treatment was precise and efficient. It was almost as though the nation was apologising for its previous lack of hospitality. Procedures went purposefully on.

Radiation treatment brought rapid loss of hair. Chemical therapy came next. Each day walking became more difficult. Eyesight faded almost completely in one eye and double vision set in, in both. In the face of all this, the patient seemed set on continuing life as long as possible.

Hospital food was a distinct bonus as it was far superior to prison food. M1611 was hungry most of the time now. There were also more people to meet.

A social worker came and went. So too did a tall and sombre Anglican clergyman. Other patients talked to M1611 and he learnt more English.

Weeks passed slowly after the initial surgery. He seemed much stronger and a casual observer may not have guessed that he was about to die.

But it was an Indian summer. His eyes were the first symptoms of further decay. Images quickly became even more ill defined. Then his body started to decline.

Movement was a painful and uncertain task. Eventually even his mind began to play tricks on him. He was heavily sedated when before his eyes came what seemed an obvious illusion.

It was just after his final visit to the radiation ward and he was on the fringe of sleep when a different visitor sat beside his bed. It was Mirinda. She was off duty.

Suddenly she was there. She had slipped silently beside him like a shadow. She watched him sleep. A long time passed but still she stayed.

When he awoke, he reached out for her. She took his hand.

'I suddenly happy!' he cried almost loudly.

His palliative silence was broken with his laughter.

'Thank you for being here. I love you. You marry me?'

She simply smiled.

'Thank you thank you thank you for being here.'

She kept on smiling and gently squeezed his hand.

'It's all right,' she said. 'My pleasure.'

Abruptly he drifted back into sleep. She stayed with him until late in the night.

Mirinda became a regular feature of his room during the few days that followed. They shared little bursts of conversation from time to time. When speaking became too difficult for M1611, she began to tell him stories.

Stories of the Dreamtime, of the talking tracks, of the trees, of the creatures, of the stars, of the winds, of the rivers, of the mountains. More stories of danger, of fear, of magic and love.

He listened in peace to her gentle voice, occasionally murmuring approval. Her gestures, facial expression and the light in her eyes helped compensate for the words he did not understand.

'Will you marry me?' he would say from time to time. A silent smile was her constant reply. Until the last story of the last day before the hospital staff agreed that there was nothing more they could do for him at this stage of his illness. She spoke very softly.

'Yes,' she said.

M1611 closed his eyes. Despite his pain, he felt the stirrings of love. She knew, and squeezed his hand.

Dearest Laura, out-of-the-ordinary things have a habit of occurring unexpectedly. Unpredictable things. This story is about a compassion that crossed barriers of distance and existence and time. It was Mirinda who decided to bring her love to M1611.

In some way she had come to understand the truth of his situation. Something had awakened the spirit of this young woman from the oldest of cultures, a spirit that knew no age or season. Perhaps it was the mysterious music of the ages that brought them together. We can never know.

Nor can we know what subtle administrative procedures lay behind the marriage approval. Somewhere in the labyrinth of regulations, someone found ways of persuading authority to act. In some mystic manner the empathy of a civil servant made M1611's dream come true.

Mirinda and M1611 were wed in a civil ceremony, before a mainly medical congregation. It was a painful time for the man, but he seemed to find strength from somewhere. He gave his vows slowly in a wheelchair.

The bride wore simple white and her dark beauty moved observers. Respectful joy erupted gently as the marriage service ended.

The next day saw them in a little motel overlooking the sea. From a balcony, man and wife watched the waves catch their breath and then dance on the sand of the beach.

A fisherman was cleaning his catch in a small boat near the shore. M1611 thought how lucky the fisherman was to be free. Seagulls hovered nearby, noisily awaiting the discarded scraps. The birds too were free.

Mirinda stood beside the wheelchair.

'It's the spirit of the sea,' she softly said to her new husband. 'It gives man food. But only enough as the man needs, no more, because it also loves its creatures.'

'I love you as much as sea loves its creatures,' said M1611, wincing just a little with the pain.

'I love you too,' she said

They kept on looking from the balcony at the world around them.

'And the spirits of the land,' she continued, 'the trees, the rivers, the hills. They are all our friends. Can you see how they are welcoming you in this sunshine. Close your eyes and you will see them.'

'Yes I see them,' he said with closed eyes.

'And the animals. They are our friends. We guard them. But we have lost many. Some are no more seen by white men. Some don't even have white men's names, only tribal names, because they died even before white men found them.'

'Sad. Yes that very sad. Too late for me to love them. But I still love you.'

'I love you too. That wind is getting stronger. We'd better go inside.'

She wheeled him back into the shelter of the room and made some coffee.

'I very lucky,' he said.

She held his hand and they sat together for quite a long time, not speaking but just looking at each other. Then she helped him onto the bed. Soon he was asleep.

She covered him and tucked him in. Then she went back out onto the balcony and watched the fisher-man a little longer, and the birds, and the gently rolling ocean.

The two stayed in the motel for three more days. They did not talk much. Occasionally they laughed at a mistake he made with English or just simply because of the joy of their togetherness. On the third day his health declined sharply.

'I know I not stay much longer,' he struggled to say, looking deeply into her eyes. But you and me are one happy person. Thank you very much.'

She could see it was time again for the hospital.

His hospital bed lay beneath a small bunch of native flowers. M1611 was now in the morphine stage. Mirinda knew that their remaining time was limited. Two doctors quietly confirmed her thoughts.

The next day was his last. In the final stage he lay peacefully on the bed breathing heavily even though, as Mirinda knew, his life had virtually ended. She stroked his head and sang gently some of her favourite childhood songs. At the end of one of her songs, M1611 died.

Mirinda came to this internment-centre just once to look around after he died. She came, we shared the story, and then she left for far away.

Today, I am feeling very sad. Maybe I should give in to my persecutors, to get some peace before I die. Perhaps not.

Last well my precious flower.

M1611 has gone now forever from this place

Narni.

* * * * *

And the animals. They are our friends.

IX

Something Shall Come of Nothing

Law is a flag, and gold is the wind that makes it wave.

— Russian Proverb

Dearest Laura
Who Leads Me Along The Path To Forever,

I am sick today and cannot eat my food. There is nowhere to gain respite, and nothing to do but wait.

Sometimes heroes are not models of action but simply those who wait for more opportune times. If we dare to look, heroes can be found in the oddest places.

There is a found-hero in this neighbourhood. I have not yet told you about the man with no number who fought his enemies with peace. It is a curious story.

I call him Nemo, because he has never been a prisoner here and so has no number. Yet he has been a visitor, in a very strange way. I will tell you his story as I understand it.

* * * * *

Nemo's life was spectacular from its very beginnings. He was born into a rich and influential family. Although he was a good man, the enemies of his family were everywhere, in the guise of competitors.

In his birthplace where he lived, social change was gradually but relentlessly accelerating. Power was becoming respected more than life itself.

The élite rulers had discovered that the best way to gain control over people was to create fear and then pretend to have the solution. Always, that solution involved hatred, killing and where possible, a boost to the economy. Weapons are well known as the most powerful and lucrative boost of all. To the careful observer, it was obvious that the biggest producers of weapons were fighting the longest wars.

Nemo thought about these things. He had been a thinker and a keen observer from his childhood years.

When the child grew to manhood and saw through a glass darkly, he noted that his enemies treated him as a fortunate, wealthy and powerful rival who should be defeated. But he remained always sharp and intelligent, and soon became their master in business, buying and selling with remarkable skill.

A financial empire seemed to fall effortlessly into place. The trouble with this successful man was he had a conscience. He was a kind of shady-deals-detector and his favourite pastime was to outbid the villains.

As a result, in the jungle of free enterprise, opportunists watched his every move and tried to anticipate his latest plans with a view to ultimate conquest. They were desperate to protect their interests. They formed consortia against him. They set financial traps for him.

But always he was one triumphant step ahead of them. As a result, he became even richer.

So life for him was happy and in many ways free of tension. His employees tended to call life 'a breeze' and they were glad to be under his wing.

Each day ticked over effortlessly and comfortably for this man. The almost boring monotony continued until one unexpected event that changed things dramatically. A death transformed his life and helped him get to know himself better than ever before.

Nemo was walking alone through a teeming, glossy shopping mall. He was on a mission for new clothes appropriate to a forthcoming business conference. He found himself walking past a very old man holding up a magazine for sale. It was one of those publications whose circulation was designed to give homeless people a job as sellers, and a small income.

Nemo stopped and looked at the old man. The face reminded him vaguely of the Dead Sea Scrolls. It was wrapped in grey, curly hair that covered his time-worn ears. The hands that held out the magazines were gnarled branches of an old tree.

'G'day mate,' the seller said. 'Read all about it. Just a few dollars.' He winked and smiled, ' And a bite for the needy.'

Nemo reached for his wallet, took out five dollars and handed the note to the old man.

'Thank you very much,' he said. 'Good going to you mate. Have a good day.'

With those few words the old man suddenly clutched his chest and fell dead at Nemo's feet. A heart attack was the medical diagnosis. The old man had been struggling with health as well as poverty and depression for several years.

That event did strange things to Nemo. Mind-sweeping things.

The presence of death tends to sharpen every mind. Nemo remembered his childhood hero Phil Ochs, and his song *There But For Fortune*. More significantly he began to have inexplicable feelings of guilt about his own vast wealth by comparison with the poor. Or was it anger rather than guilt?

Whatever the reason, Nemo suddenly turned on his heels and ended his journey to Damascus.

On a sudden impulse, he converted everything he owned into cash and walked away from stocks and bonds, leaving his business empire to be fought over by the wolves of corporations. He sold it to them for the price of their greed.

Strangely, his actions seemed to make him richer still. Then he began to lose faith in stocks and shares, so he converted most of his fortune into capital-guaranteed bonds, stored in unobserved safety beyond the hills of Switzerland.

Then he threw away the usual garments of a businessman: dark striped suits flagging importance and shoes that reflected your acquisitive face. As others saw it, he suddenly became an eccentric. He brought gasps for a time by dressing in an unobtrusive toga, like a time traveller from ancient Rome.

He changed his life into simple things. He started catching trains and buses. Sandals replaced his sparkling shoes, and in them he walked the streets of country towns and cities day and night, making notes.

Occasionally he attracted the attention of the media. The occasional journalist wrote stories about Nemo. Mostly however, Nemo remained nobody.

The unobtrusive non-conformist then decided for fun, to carry with him a homespun shoulder bag in all his meanderings. That was when another alarming deviancy emerged. Chrometophobia or fear of money, the world's most rare disease, almost had him in its clutches.

To ease this pain he placed bulky bundles of two-dollar coins that he called 'pieces of eight' in his shoulder bag. He then constantly did his best every day, to find needy cases to give the 'eight' to. He became a kind of minstrel-like street performer. From time to time he would call out in the oddest places: 'New lives for old! New lives for old!' People usually turned their heads and walked on in embarrassed indifference, preoccupied as they were with higher things.

In the cities especially, the ordinary people had grown used to loud-mouthed deviants wandering the streets expounding non sequiturs, especially at election time. Nemo felt triumph in his awareness that he was not like them.

His mind's mission statements were so different from those of the entrepreneur he once was. He imposed a veil of ignorance on himself about tomorrow. He saw a whole world in need of change and not just his own narrow destiny. He would study this world, and find solutions. Then happiness would follow, whatever disasters he might meet.

Nemo became obsessed with a battery of other crazy dreams. They took his mind everywhere . . . to runaway children, sleepers on park benches, women of the night, and even wandering dogs. He had visions of a new and better existence for all of them.

Hospitals came into his mind as well, available to all with comfortable beds instead of chairs in crowded emergency waiting rooms. In his new havens of hope an unbalanced budget would always be better than a death.

He dreamed of little corner stores, formerly manipulated out of existence by corporate food giants, suddenly coming back. Real shopkeepers and not television fantasies.

And there were the farmers. Farmers who had found spades and ploughs turned into iron traps of vertical growers' contracts with big business. Now he saw their farms mystically transformed into tree-filled channels of coolness with organic seeds and freedom to sell their produce lovingly whenever and wherever they wished.

In his dreams there were more and more lonely old people abruptly finding reassurance and care instead of depersonalised abandonment in heartless hostels which their life savings had to pay for.

He saw schools in his mind's eye, magically finding graffiti-free walls and grassy space instead of treeless asphalt, for their children to exist on. And families kept together.

Visiting Day

Ah Laura! This was a dangerous man. He had the capacity to destroy the modus operandi of the Western world.

This apparent folly, hidden delusions of reform, took charge of him. Obsession grew and grew.

He went to university lectures instead of business conferences. He became a student of everything. He studied with fanatical dedication history, literature, physics, chemistry, engineering, the Law and even the theatre.

Dearest Laura, apart from the menace of humorous satire, there is nothing more dangerous to ruling élites than a university. It was there, in the oldest university of the land, that Nemo drew the last straw.

As part of his newfound studies, he published a paper on endocrine disrupters. You may not know this, but these widely unheralded recent discoveries are used surreptitiously in many products to increase profit, often by reducing costs. But no one is sure of the potential harm they may do. They can, it seems, in many ways be potential destroyers of people.

Now Nemo's papers on climate change and other critiques of mankind's follies had brought him enemies too, but this latest publication was his most dangerous deed ever.

Unimagined storm clouds suddenly loomed over the horizon of his life. Changes beyond even his control.

After this apparent exposé by him, violence threatened everywhere. His life instantly became a vast danger to the establishment. This act of his was the fuse of the dynamite required to blow him out of existence.

The man was cool however. He had friends, good advisers who warned him about approaching troubles.

When the brakes of his Mercedes inexplicably failed and he was almost killed, he began to take the warnings seriously. Then when his country retreat, where he would have been staying but for the sudden illness of his Aunty Thel, was burnt to the ground, awareness set in. The warnings were becoming verified and the dangers clearer.

He realised that integrity in business is sometimes more deadly than take-over bids by foreign consortia. He knew that his future was suddenly in real trouble. It was time for urgent action.

This man was a brilliant planner. Things were always, with Nemo, carefully assessed. He was not given to half measures.

With the help of a few trusted friends, he devised a remarkable solution. It was linked of all things, to life after death. It was an escape undreamed of by Nemo's enemies.

Newspaper headlines, one startling day, trumpeted that Nemo's car, shoes and other personal items had been found at the cliff top of the Gap in Sydney's Watsons Bay. Was this possible? Could this brilliantly successful man have danced on the air beyond the edge of the lofty cliffs and killed himself?

No trace of his life was subsequently found in any of the world's four corners. And details of Swiss banks were inaccessible. This odd man seemed validly to be dead.

The apparent death evoked stories in several newspapers and tributes from former business associates. His passing was mourned publicly by many people especially his most active enemies.

There was quite a fracas for a time. Then, as so often happens, demigods are easily replaced and forgotten.

During the brief period of mourning over his non-existent death, the distinguished former man of boardrooms whisked himself into another identity. The plastic surgery was undemanding, as a dead man needs but minor changes. It was a brilliant success. He was now a different man, and free to undertake a new journey under different stars.

His face was not the only thing to change. History became his inviolable sounding board for future deeds. Nemo II was born in the cities of his mind.

He tried always to be positive, although significant grievances from the past still lingered. He continued to see the law as an ass owned and fed by the rich. He still winced when he heard the most powerful of autocrats praising freedom and democracy as they organised unilateral declarations of war. But somehow he felt these matters would eventually take care of themselves.

He had more important things to do. He sprang forth in a new direction. And what a change it was! When the curtain went up, his own version of ethical business began.

With his new face, skill with disguise and enough money to make showmen pinch themselves with delight, he decided to create, of all things, a clandestine, cloak-and-dagger theatre company.

He set about this task with astonishing speed.

What he made was not a theatre or 'seeing place' as we know it. It was instead a covert organisation that the players named in their secret journals: *The Comedie Australaise.*

It was all an undercover adventure. Nemo and his carefully recruited, willing actors found roles to play among real people in carefully chosen, true-to-life scenarios. In each case, the sole artistic purpose was to end injustice. Dario Fo rides on.

That was how Nemo, the former archetypal entrepreneur, and now a master of disguise and performance, was able gently to weave himself into
powerful places of action; to set in train sweeping
changes, and then fade away into the mists of
mystery. That was how he came to visit this detention-centre.

Dearest Laura computer gimmickry is always
welcomed by institutions, especially when it replaces
human labour that has become so costly. This
establishment was no exception.

Konnichi Wa, computer specialist from the company
Magic Menus, seemed to the Centre management a
most fortunate discovery to overhaul their technical
systems. And his price-scale was most attractive. In
the privatised world, the title 'expert' opens doors to
all kinds of significant places. Expensive experts
cross boundaries easily.

Konichi Wa with his cast of three who arrived out of
the dust one Friday at noon in a bright red van with
pink wheels, was in reality beginning a new performance by *The Comedie Australaise.*

The driver was ushered towards a suitable parking
space. He and his two assistants were welcomed by
two uniformed men and given unchallenged entry to
the Centre. It was an obvious mission of service.

They came. They worked. They left.

But O my Laura! What they left behind.

Soon after their departure, graffiti was found on every switchboard in doorways and in other surprising places. The same message was repeated many times, It read simply: **Mandatory Detention Sucks.**

The Management was furious. They made venomous enquiries in vain. The mystery remained unsolved. Federal police were informed. Magic Menus was investigated by the Law. Vigorous enquiries meant the sting was quickly revealed. But there were no clues for restitution. Konnichi Wa and his company simply did not exist outside the barbed wire of this detention centre.

Normal life appeared to return to the institution in the days that followed. But seven midnights later, the second phase began. The dark silence was blown apart.

The Centre's sirens sprang into life and violently shattered the night. The traditional alarm for an escape.

Guards came running from everywhere, some in pyjamas. Shouts rang around the camp. Searchlights split the darkness. Fences were examined. Rolls were checked. The prison was frantically circumnavigated. Nothing came of it. There had been no escape.

An hour later: Phase 3. The silence was violently assaulted once more, this time by the PA system beginning a steady, sonorous roll call of every refugee who had entered the centre since its opening years before. The fate of each: death, deportation, release was loudly announced to the night. When the list was completed, the roll call began again.

After an hour of extreme discord, the chaos withered slowly back into silence. Nobody could find the mechanism behind the strange events. The camp executives spent countless sleepless moments pondering about possible causes.

A computer virus was suspected but could not be found. Eventually, routines returned to normal although there was some anxiety about further trouble.

At precisely midnight one week later, the anxiety was justified. Phase 4. The noise came back. This time it was music. The music was *Swing Low, Sweet Chariot* followed by *When The Saints Come Marching In* and *Nobody Knows The Trouble I've Seen* and *The Stars and Stripes Forever* in constant replay mode. It was so loud that even the birds of the night flew away in fear.

The din lasted much longer this time. No matter what they did, technicians could not stop it. The CEO and his staff once more ran through the halls in confusion. At last the sounds ceased. As before, nobody could find a better possible cause than a computer virus.

The next day was marked with enquiries and further extensive recriminations. A deep sense of unease and discord seized the minds of the establishment managers.

The inmates were more amused than angry. We began to wonder what would happen next. Some of us stayed awake until the next midnight. Somehow we knew there was more to come.

We were not disappointed; only surprised by the extent of the chaos. Phase 5. At the very witching hour, every computer run device: fax machines, telephones, stoves, washing machines, word processors, photocopiers, television sets, digital speakers and even electronic kettles, sprang into life.

We, the prisoners, could feel the institution crumbling around us. It was like the fall of the Bastille and the collapse of the **Ancien Régime** to us.

Important people as well as we lesser mortals were beginning to experience destructive sleep deprivation.

Actually, for us it was also a satisfying feeling of delight. We were starting to see clearly the point of it all. The following day, there was extensive coverage in several newspapers, including even *The New York Times*.

Many letters, I believe, then found their way into the Australian Press discussing the comparative value of detention-centres, temporary protection visas and work permits.

There were political repercussions too. The prime minister apparently became involved. He hovered between a state of emergency and a phone call to the White House, but in the end did nothing. Some people are saying outside this place, that the Konichi affair will have significant future electoral significance.

It was some time before the harsh reality of normality returned to us. I was told by a friendly guard that repercussions were felt across the seas.

In this country, the total cost of enquiries and other action was apparently many thousands of dollars, or more. As for the prisoners, all we did was observe from our wire-bound cocoons with placid, interested eyes. And then it was over. Those eyes of ours by this had seen the last of the strange events. But we would remember Konichi. Especially after the written words I found behind my cell door. Somehow, he had heard of me.

Here was our hero, our man of many faces. Here was our benign terrorist. Not a terrorist but an *errorist*. A gentle trickster who used the system to teach lessons where they were most needed.

The red faces he caused could be seen as the out-comes of foolish behaviour. Undoubtedly these events improved security. They probably also injected some wisdom into administrative thought processes. And there was no loss of life.

But there was loss of status for questionable government policies and probable loss of votes. The usual suspects were rounded up.

Government advertisements were quickly produced alerting citizens to the ever-increasing danger of terrorism. Konichi's likeness, the face of a non-existent character, was produced for inclusion on warning signs for refrigerator magnets. The production of these devices was doubled.

I wondered deeply where the secret company would next perform. I was curious as to whether there had been other performances previously, somewhere. I really could not tell. So I simply returned with a slight smile to my own solitude.

Konnichi Wa has gone now forever from this place. But fine influences from elsewhere eventually will scorn our borders.

With love,

Narni.

* * * * *

But fine influences from elsewhere,
eventually will scorn our borders.

IX

Romeo, Romeo! Therefore art thou Romeo

Let him kiss me with the kisses of his mouth: for thy love is better than wine.

— The Song of Solomon I, 2

Dearest Laura,
Child of All Love Everywhere,

I have been placed in solitary again, this time for two weeks. I must fight on, but peacefully. My love for you is my only means of survival. Love Laura, is wherever you find it. But what is love?

M1432 was in love with love. There were kisses in his mind. Flirting eyes. Dancing curly locks of hair. Silken breasts. Hands that caressed. Soft breathing that came and went.

What else can a lonely man dream of? M1432 was a very lonely man when he came here, because he was a lover in a land of hate. In his own country too, he longed for love and for many more friends. Those friends he had, knew he was an addicted optimist.

'Everything happens for the best,' was his constant cry, no matter what happened to him.

He needed to believe in miracles. In spite of the evidence around him, he had complete trust in fate and waited eagerly for good things to happen. Otherwise he would have succumbed to the chaos.

On top of this, he had an ardent sense of beauty. He saw poetry everywhere. He was a keen student of the world, always asking questions. Why was the sky blue? What music did birds dance to? How do ants know it is about to rain?

He talked about everything with enthusiasm. His mind was part of an adventurous spirit and his words constantly bubbled like a mountain stream. When people listened to him they were were usually charmed.

As a citizen of his battered city where every day was shattered by bombs and whistling shells and falling buildings and screams of fear and cries of pain, what else was left to do but dream? The devastation was a hard burden for M1432 because he had a tenderness for living things, both great and small.

That was why he followed another dream across the sea.

On the boat to Australia, he sang songs of happiness in the Bosnian tongue, although he spoke very good

English. There was considerable seasickness in the decrepit, almost unseaworthy boat, but M1432 was a good sailor. Instead of vomiting, he steadfastly dreamed of a new and happy life that he believed was bound to come his way. What else was there to do?

A beautiful wife, laughing children, sunshine and a farm filled his thoughts. He dared to imagine these things happening because, in spite of everything bad around him, he believed they would appear in his life. Destiny was his friend, how else could he have escaped from his war-torn home and be heading for his new life?

But dreams are ephemeral things. Something happened towards the end of that voyage which savagely tested his optimism.

A naval patrol-boat coming out of the morning mist, ordered their boat to stop. This was a vast problem for an optimist.

He quickly pulled an ancient, hand-made bottle--a childhood souvenir--from his tattered coat pocket. Deftly he produced from another pocket, a slightly crumpled big close-up of himself, which he had had a friend take just before the war broke out. Frantical-ly he wrote on the back of the photo:

> *Ladies who find this photo come to me. I will ask you to be my bride.*

Carefully rolling the photo to make it fit, he thrust it into the bottle and added the cork. Unobtrusively he slipped his arm over the side not visible to the patrol-boat crew, and committed his message to the ocean. What else was there for him to do?

Just in time. Soon all passengers were arrested and some of them, including M1432, eventually found themselves in this internment place.

Now Laura, a sealed bottle is one of the most seaworthy containers there is. There are currents in the sea that are so powerful that they rule the weather of whole continents. And bottles ride these currents better than ocean liners.

This one, launched by M1432, bobbed its way merrily around the coast for many months. It weathered storms, dancing like a ballerina on the foam.

Sometimes it lay becalmed like a painted bottle upon a painted ocean. It bobbed and weaved like a boxer fighting for a title. And then finally, as if weary of travel, it beached itself on an island close to the Australian coast.

I must tell you this island is not an ordinary piece of land. It is a pure and fertile place especially famous for its milk and cream. Because of this fecundity it is inhabited by many birds and an industrious group of happy and successful business people. One of these island citizens is Rosie.

Now Rosie is a strong and important woman. Born eight decades ago, she is still the mother of the island. Nothing there escapes her notice.

The waves are her friends. She speaks to them every day as she walks along the beaches.

It was almost as if the Fates knew this when they brought the bottle to her, guiding its dance across the curling waters of the tiny beach and, at precisely the right moment, bringing the bobbing glass unerringly to her notice.

She saw the flash amidst the waves. She watched it tumbling over and over in the foam until it lay a short distance from her feet. She paused like a bird above its prey, having interrupted her usual after-noon walk, lifted her skirts and picked up the bottle. Her eyes were still notable for their unerring scrutiny.

She held the small bottle up to the sky, examining the contents with worldly interest. With interest in her eye, like a spy from the Kremlin, she carefully removed the cork. Then, with both eyes narrowing, she extracted and examined the photograph. Slowly she turned it over and read the message.

For a moment, she lifted her head and looked omnisciently at the horizon, as if to traverse the samite of the sea and take in the other side of the earth from whence the bottle had come. A smile flickered across her face. A light came into her eyes. A magic bottle, she thought.

Several seagulls had by this time joined her. Some hovered motionless in the air above her head. Others encircled her on the sand. All of them eyed her meticulously with a strange familiarity.

Rosie stayed a few moments longer. Then she put the photo back and sealed the bottle. The young man's face stayed in her mind as she turned to confront the breeze once more, and resumed her walk. The seagulls rose as one to ride that wind, and went about their business.

When the old woman returned home, she opened the little white gate with unusual vigour. There was a spring in her step which belied her age, as she hurried along the winding white path past the lemon tree and the Valencia orange and the plum tree, into the little white house. Rosie had a plan.

Now life on this island, remote as its location is from the big cities, might be assumed to dull the wit of its inhabitants. You might see Rosie in your first predictions as unsophisticated, rural and compliant.

If you did, you would be in line for a very rude awakening. For Rosie is tranquility recollected in emotion. She is most definitely a woman of the world. A survivor. A weatherer of storms. A believer in the power of enterprise.

Rosie had good reason for this belief. There is little doubt that without her acumen and courage, this world-famous island, this fountain of rural energy, would have become a refresher course venue for Robinson Crusoe.

This woman had always known that inferiority is a state of mind and not a genetic outcome. Through her own strength, she became used to winning battles with developers, with public authorities, with politicians and, more importantly, with Nature's elements around her.

The old woman of the sea was not only a shrewd and calculating business icon. She was the mother of philosophy. Rosie knew that simple answers are always wrong. It takes little time to fool a fool. So she became a cunning and careful planner. Important details were never too small.

In addition to all of this, she was an indelible romantic. On that day, her ocean had brought a mysterious young man into her life and she was determined to find him. Opportunity rocks.

So Rosie surged into action. She dressed herself in her most civic-minded clothes. She bought her ticket from the island to the mainland and another to the city. Amidst the beauty of one of the island's spring mornings, armed with her characteristic look of determination, she set off on her mission.

A whole day passed. She knocked on many depart-
mental doors in the city until finally she found
sustenance at the office of the Department of
Immigration. They told her it would be necessary for
her to travel to the Federal Capital. So she prepared
for this.

A week later she was there. In library archives she
found stories. And there was a photo. His photo. She
knew the date of the arrest of her young man from
the newspaper cuttings. This greatly helped her
search. She dealt with unenthusiastic bureaucrats
enthusiastically.

Even so, she had to return to Canberra three times.
Finally she found the most likely location of the
young man's internment. It was here, in my prison.

Then came the next stage of her quest. By this time
three months had passed.

The journey to this internment-centre was too far for
the old woman. So, through her aggressive negotiat-
ing style and by pulling strings with friends in
Rotary International, Rosie arranged a meeting with
a high official from the internment-centre at an office
in the city of Aridity.

Her story was that there was a strong chance that the
young man in the photo was a distant member of her
own family and his interests were in her heart. The
photo, she implied, was an incredible family

resemblance. As any successful entrepreneur will tell you, truth can be a powerful ally when it is stretched a little.

Then came her masterstroke. Rosie, woman of the world, sovereign of the fields, provider of milk and cream to many institutions throughout the state, was a mistress of business intercourse. Therefore she knew the power of the Press.

Cagily, she increased her bargaining power by telling the official that a journalist from *The Advertiser* was deeply interested in her remarkable story. This part of her account was in fact true.

Such a story would be a powerful way she knew, of adding status to the hitherto appalling reputation of the refugee prison. Would the official, in the light of this exciting situation, be so kind as to endeavour to match the photograph with a person at the internment-centre? The strategy worked.

In one week's time, Rosie received a phone call on the island from the CEO of the centre. Yes. A match had been found. The young man was held in this centre.

The woman of the world wasted no time. A meeting was arranged. This time the long journey to the centre was considered essential. A hire car and a travelling companion made the journey possible. It took two days.

In the mid-morning of that second wonderful day, M1432 in the CEO's office, met Rosie and her travelling companion Ellenie. There are no words adequate for the prisoner's joy. For Rosie, it was love at second sight. A deep, motherly love for her genie of the bottle.

More importantly, two other pairs of eyes met--with interesting results. M1432 looked handsome, despite his prison garb. Ellenie was drawn to the smile she had not seen on the photograph.

For the young man, there were Ellenie's curls to notice, playfully dancing above the eyes. The skin, as much as could be observed outside the simple and bountiful dress she wore, was pure and sun-tanned from much farm work. The voice was lively and kind and interesting. A miracle was unfolding.

They talked excitedly to each other from the start: about farming, about trees, sunsets, songs, birds and children. It was a happy first meeting.

Rosie looked at them and smiled. You could tell that things might well be starting to fall into place. She still believed in magic.

What happened next was something far more powerful than prestidigitation. Rosie turned her sights on the channels of administration.

As soon as the meeting ended, phone calls mingled with lawyers who mingled with Ministers of the Crown who mingled with The Press. The mills of government action characteristically grind very slowly. But not when Rosie is around.

A marriage took place on the island within five weeks. The Immigration Laws were praised and reinforced.

Ellenie and M1342 went to live with Rosie on the island within daily sight of the seas that had set both of them free. The story of the bottle made wonderful copy in many countries around the world.

In five months time, yes five months, all of the young man's yearning for a farm and a family came much closer to fulfilment when Ellenie enriched his life with a beautiful baby daughter.

'Everything happens for the best,' he said. 'And every child brings hope to today, and a smile to tomorrow.'

M1342 has gone now forever from this place.

With love,

Narni

* * * * *

XI

Terror Nullius

Ars est celare artem.
True art conceals itself.

— Ovid

Dearest Laura,
Whose Skin Is White As Snow,

They have just kept me awake for five nights in my cell by not switching off my light. But I have survived Laura. And I can smell change in the air.

Your love is helping me. My keepers here constantly ask me questions about things I know nothing of. I wanted to die in those early years, so that my soul could find peace in the darkness. Now I have grown more used to the ways of this place. I have weathered most of the storms. That is my story unfolding. Here is another part of it.

* * * * *

Souls have no colour, either black or white, despite what some poets say. M1331 was a strange and unexpected companion here of a different colour.

He is an Inuk. The word just means 'a person' in his language. That is, as the word tells me, he is simply a person from the original race of a distant land. The plural is *Inuit*. Why he was here I do not know. I think he was in trouble in his own country trying to stop the hunting of seals. He has a dark complexion, but O the light in his eyes is bright.

Several days ago, strange events conspired to take him away. This is the story.

He was from the first a prisoner who attracted attention. Newspapers were drawn to his story. He became a focus of interest and action. A man from the snow in the desert sold papers.

Out of one sleepy morning in the past, a noisy crowd, mostly made up of white strangers, came and stood outside the wires of this establishment. Some of the people had long hair and some had none at all.

Some had headbands and beards, and others were not yet in the realm of puberty. And they all liked singing. They had come from many miles to stand outside this prison. My friend from afar was the reason.

The first sign of their approach was a puff of dust in the distance. Then their noise crescendoed and the dust billowed from the tramp of many, many feet. They arrived, in cars and buses and on foot, as a doppler rumble.

'Visa! Visa! Visa!' they cried with drum beat consistency. In no time they were clustered outside the main entrance. It seems they were protesting against the nature of M1331's detention, because his name was on many placards.

There were other banners too, some large and some small bearing many messages. The largest was JUSTICE HAS NO BORDERS! Others read REFUGEES CANNOT BE ILLEGALS! and THERE IS NO QUEUE!

Many tunes flowed from their mouths: *Peace Train. Nobody Knows The Trouble I've Seen. From Little Things Big Things Grow. We Shall Not Be Moved. All Men Are Brothers. We Shall Overcome.* There were many more songs of dissent--a ceaseless potpourri.

Authorities mingled authoritatively with the crowd. Uniforms were everywhere. Two intrepid young outsiders, wearing gloves, cut the barbed wires beside the gate and pulled down part of the fence.

Then violence came. Cameras opened their lenses. A line of mounted guards surged into the crowd. Some protesters were dragged by conquering guards across the dust. Other adventurous intruders tried to leap the barbs of the wire and were trapped in its tangles. A woman's voice could be heard shouting over and over: 'The whole world is watching!'

The inmates watched and cheered from time to time. The uniforms took two main activists away. The other demonstrators stayed and sang more songs.

The invasion lasted. For three days and two nights they remained. Then, as suddenly as they came, they left. All became suddenly silent, except for the birds.

In the twilight of that third day, M1331 came to me very excited. He held the blackest, smoothest stone in his hand. He gave it to me.

'It's a sorry stone,' he said. 'It was given to me by a stranger who mysteriously appeared in the courtyard this morning. I don't know where he came from. Suddenly he was there.'

I looked at its dark infinity in my hand. It was like holding a piece of the night, and yet something about it made me at peace with tomorrow. So flat and round and smooth and confidently serene. It welcomed my grasp, a gentle and unobtrusive thing, and seemed to take my eyes, beyond the hateful walls of this prison, to welcoming laughter.

'Whatever sorry means,' M1331 went on, 'that stone seemed to give me strength and freedom from fear. I think he must have been a tribal man from this country, like the tribal men of my country. I have seen such people before in my homeland.

'He gave this stone to me with a smile and said, "Take this sorry stone, O brother from a distant land. Take it and smile upon it. All will be well in the end." He then disappeared like the mist of the morning. No one could tell me how he came or went.'

M1331 went too, and left me to my thoughts.

That particular night was long. The stars seemed weary, as if longing to come down to earth. The moon was labouring like a washerwoman hanging out her clouds in the sky.

In the midst of the night we were all awakened by patterns of deep, rhythmic chanting, beating and humming, faint at first and then growing ever louder. It was as if even the trees were singing with deep wooden voices.

These strange, illegal harmonies controlled the air and wove adornments in the wind. The rhythm of a dance by dancers unseen in the night grew ever faster and their shadows seemed to fling ghostly patterns over the stars. Something was adrift in the night. A fanfare of change.

The protesters came back with the morning. They had suddenly become a multitude. I looked through the wires with wonder at the bright costumes of many nations and the black dancers.

There seemed to be more than a thousand, this time with four-wheel drive vehicles and television cameras. The noise trebled. There were microphones and a multitude of speakers. I heard them through the barbed walls around me.

After a time, the CEO with several other apparently important people walked through the gates to talk to the crowd. A small group of leaders emerged from the throng and began a very lively discussion.

One of them was a very tall, thin man with very black hair and a lithe, rhythmic body. When he walked he seemed to dance across the dust. He turned towards me for a moment and his eyes touched mine. His smile sparkled in the sun. I knew it was M1331's stranger.

The parley continued for almost an hour. I noticed the tall stranger step away from the negotiators and stand apart. He began to sing a deep rhythmic song. His feet moved in time with his singing in the subtlest of dances. Soon he returned to the group still busily discussing events.

Then came the dust.

Not from the tramp of feet this time. It was an unannounced earth-storm, suddenly conjured from the horizon. Black and red, mystic, swirling dust. Frowns of clouds wrinkled themselves from nowhere and swirled towards us. Looming first in the distance and then sweeping relentlessly over everything.

There was no escaping it. It entered your eyes. Your clothes. Doors and windows could not keep it out. The smell of it was everywhere. There was nothing left but to cover your face and shrink away from it.

The negotiators quickly broke up, took shelter in the compound and stayed there. Ends are slow in coming when you long for them.

Time and the dust eventually passed. The negotiators dispersed and the outsiders left.

Then came the wind.

Cold and bleak and crucifying. Whistling around everything. It had its own voice. Like a cackling crone.

It was as if the ancient land was chiding us. As if to say, 'Earth, fire, wind and water know no human boundaries.'

More anger came in whirlwinds, appearing from nowhere, snatching at everything that was loose. Little twisters. Rearing snakes reaching for the sky, flinging unwanted debris away in disgust. Even the sun needed to cringe incognito behind the terrified clouds.

Then came the rain.

We in the prison smelt it. It was a strange indigenous pattern, this blasphemy of nature against the gods of penal fundamentalism. The rainstorm burst upon us, hammering our walls like an avenger demanding justice.

The noise of the beating on roofs increased as the rain turned into hail. Thunder joined with lightning in the fray. Winds screamed through the wires, uprooting fence-posts and bringing down one of the watchtowers.

The tempest continued unabated. Several hours passed.

Eventually the sounds of Armageddon faded into silence. As if a signal had been given, the world gave a sigh and was suddenly still.

When that next day ended the universe seemed strangely empty, save for a small number of sha-dowy dissidents still lingering in the darkness outside the prison. These remaining demonstrators stood like contrite statues.

The figures were now peaceful, their long hair occasionally blowing in the capricious new winds. Some newsmen's cameras still continued recording. But not for long.

Eventually all of the outsiders disappeared.

The only aggressive demonstrators left were a flock of sulphur-crested cockatoos soaring and diving and hurling abuse, like anti-war activists, at the humans fixed to the ground below them.

'Far queue! Far queue!' they seemed to be saying in their high-pitched gravel voices. A few of the guards seemed impatient with the noise. One or two of the birds swooped aggressively down on them, and then swerved up and away, totally convinced of their own power.

The demonstrations had been long, dearest Laura, and, as you can see, curiously eventful.

The last event of all was even more curious. With a background of yet another setting sun, my friend M1331 walked by my cell.

To my surprise, he said goodbye. He softly told me as he passed, that he had been granted freedom and acceptance in this land. He did not fully understand why.

He had wanted me to have his sorry-stone as a parting gift, but could not find it. It had strangely vanished from his cell.

Then he whispered: 'Never mind. Let it be. My chains have fallen away!' Before I could reply, he was gone. Where, I cannot exactly tell. Nor do I know precisely why.

But quivering in my mind are questions about the dark stranger who visited him in person. Was he, the stranger, a vital part of a universal indigenous brotherhood, and in some way responsible for that release?

Was he a Clever Man? A learned child of the land, with the understanding of natural forces derived from those who have gone before over countless thousands of years in this place. Or was he just a sensitive soul able to hear the music of the earth and the air, not to control the elements, but to anticipate their whims?

And was he able somehow, to threaten our captors? Did he make them uneasy about things they could not understand? Did he create a reason to let M1331 go? I will never know.

The crowd and the cameras too are now but memories. I can see the stars again through my tiny window if I really try. The air is crinkling clear and free of dust. Flowers have come back into my dreams.

Dream with me, my Love. That some day we will be free together. M1331 has gone now forever from this place.

Narni.

* * * * *

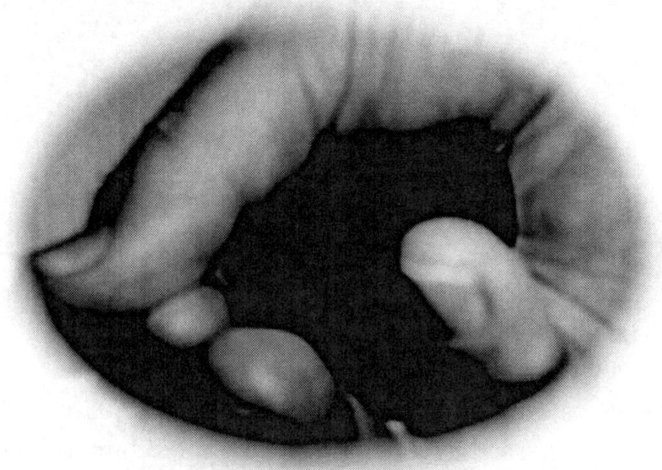

I looked at its dark infinity in my hand. It was like holding a piece of the night, and yet something about it made me at peace with tomorrow. So flat and round and smooth and confidently serene. It welcomed my grasp, a gentle and unobtrusive thing, and seemed to take my eyes, beyond the hateful walls of this prison, to welcoming laughter.

XII

Too Late!

**I have a rendezvous with Death
At some disputed barricade.**
— Alan Seeger, 1888-1916

Dearest Laura,
Who Gives Me Life,

Death is only an occasional visitor to this place. Yet once He passed by when no one expected him. It was many, many years ago at the very beginning of my detention here.

Of all our guards then, three seemed to stand apart. They were interested in no one but themselves. Never willing to listen to pleas for mercy from people in trouble. Always menacing in their black uniforms.

They were the perfect enforcers of this institution. Any internee caught breaking a curfew or straying out of bounds always seemed to meet them in the end.

Old M1111, from the cell next to mine, invented names for them. He called them The Black Guards: Mars, Ares and Thor. Bullies like them are never popular with those they control.

The reputation of these men was not slow to spread throughout the centre. And even beyond it. They were perfect instruments of power. Yet they too have their own story . . .

Destiny itself played a trick on them. One fateful day, five detainees, numbers M1441 to M1445, happened to be passing through this institution. It was a one-night stand. They were due for deportation next day. On this day before they were to leave, they found themselves in a compromising situation.

Relatively young prisoners, they were Afghans. They were quiet, had no English and wanted nothing more than to keep out of trouble. Their lives since their abortive attempts to enter the country, had been filled with anxiety. Trouble with their captors was the last event on earth they would wish for.

Yet in spite of their good intentions, they found themselves in trouble. They had strayed into a prohibited area. It happened when Thor inadvertently left a door open and they thought he was inviting them through it.

When Mars saw their apparent trespass, he seized the nearest prisoner, M1441, and drew him to within an inch of his own malevolent face. Drunk with menace, Mars spoke through clenched lips.

'Going somewhere mate?' he growled

As M1441 understood no English, he did not speak.

'What! No speak a de English?'

M1441 recoiled but still did not speak.

'All right towel-head, try this for size.' Mars launched a fore-arm jolt into the prisoner's midriff. M1441 dropped like a shot bird.

He hit his head on the ground. The guard pulled him to his feet clutching the clothing beneath the prisoner's chin, and with his gym-hardened arms lifted the struggling refugee into the air.

'Out of bounds is a dangerous place. No one can see what happens to you here.'

Mars let M1441 fall again. He put one foot menacingly on his stomach in mock triumph, without applying any weight and then pummelled him viciously as he struggled to his feet.

The overwhelmed young man crumpled once more and lay stretched out with the apparent alertness of a rag doll. Two of the other imprisoned men rushed to help him. Ares and Thor immediately surged forward and pinned each new victim to the ground, wrenching their arms into twisted crosses behind their backs.

Anger seemed to well out of the pores of the guards' skins. For those few moments they could feel and think nothing but hate. The prisoners were dehumanised, not for doing something wrong but because of the assumed menace of their alien natures.

'Keep still you fuckin' foreign bastards or we'll rip your fuckin' arms off,' yelled Thor.

Not all birds of prey have wings.

The prisoners quickly crumbled into submission and, before they knew it, they were bemoaning their wounds in the single cell that was to be their shelter for the night. It was a savage lesson well learnt, especially by the young man who had first angered Mars.

He went back to his cell with the back of his head matted with blood. He walked with a limp. And tears from his blackened eyes stained his young face. The five foreigners, about to be thrown out of this hostile land next day, consoled each other.

They talked each other through the night.

The eldest of the five, M1443, felt in his bones that the violent men needed pity, not hate. He saw them as prisoners of their own anger.

They were merely tools of animosity caught up in the agendas of their superiors. Powerful people in high places, these superiors, able to stay safe from exposure and recrimination because of blurred lines of responsibility. They would not, however, hesitate to turn The Black Guards into scapegoats if necessary, to protect more prestigious reputations.

The guards' hashish of anger seemed to grow next day, after this incident.

'These foreign bastards will be the death of us if we don't mangle 'em now,' Mars had said to his comrades after he closed the last cell door.

'Don't give 'em an inch. Grind their guts into blood and bone if necessary.' His two cohorts mumbled supportive abuse as they closed several other metal doors and then left to go about other business.

It was early morning, as The Black Guards set about their mission of deportation. The task: to take the deportees on the long journey across a virtual desert to the port city of Aridity.

Their means of transport was a prison mini-van. They would take turns at driving and when not driving, simply watch over the prisoners.

The miserable refugees, one far more miserable than the others and bruised and aching as well, lined up ready to board the vehicle. They hesitated.

'Come on you dim-witted dickheads. In you go,' growled Ares. 'We're going to an airport not a funeral,' said Thor pushing one of the refugees, 'get a move on.'

He kicked at the recalcitrant, missing flesh and hitting the metal of the door. It brought blood to his shin and foul curses to his lips.

The prisoners stared blankly without moving. Not one word was understood.

Gestures and curses and violent shoving followed. The method was effective. The inmates were soon on board.

The wounded Guard spoke to himself: 'Fuckin' Wog retards! Jesus, this job is worth more pay.' His leg was significantly damaged. The pain was considerable.

M1444 heard 'Jesus', a word he knew. It brought a fleeting anticipation of kindness to the prisoner's mind. The kindness did not come.

The journey began. The route they had to follow twisted and turned through an empty and barren section of the Australian terrain. It was cool in the early morning when they set out. But the afternoon was fiendishly hot. And the distance was long. Very long.

Their road was a road in name only. Dusty, pot-holed and unfrequented, it promised trouble. In many places the surface was better beside the road than on it. The group of hate-weary prisoners and their short-tempered captors passed uncomfortably through the morning, almost against the wishes of the vehicle.

The old mini-bus had just been serviced but even so, the vehicle was feeling the heat as it began to climb over a range of low hills. They had almost reached the bottom of the last, relatively steep hill when, as if on a sudden whim, the brakes gave way. The vehicle accelerated at a frightening speed, Mars clenching the wheel with his massive hands. One of the wheels hit a pothole that seemed to the passengers an offspring of the Grand Canyon.

There was an appalling grind and concussion as the vehicle lurched out of control. The irresistible momentum continued until, with gunshot sudden-ness, an axle broke and the van plunged into a small ravine.

The world inverted itself. Trees seemed to be hanging from the sky and dust polluted everything. The crunch and grind of metal sounded doubly loud in the midst of all their fear.

The mini disaster was not fatal although it played minor havoc with limbs. Bodies escaped relatively well, but all communication-equipment was shattered into an inoperative mess. The large water container they needed was smashed into small pieces and its contents sank into the thirsty ground.

The curses of the guards rang out but, as usual, the passengers did not understand the language. The dust settled between groans and expletives . . .

Thus began a very long walk. There was no choice. A waterless struggle across parched earth amidst fiery heat was all that was left to them. The first thing they noticed was the peculiar redness of the soil. The heat bounced off it like silent curses.

The landscape was very dry. In places it had degenerated almost to desert. Troubles followed closely on their heels.

When you cannot see your destination even though you might have optimistic thoughts, circles are no different from straight lines. The walkers soon became lost in a fiery maze of confusion.

On they staggered, Laura, under the vengeful sun. A watchful eagle hovered majestically above them, hanging ten on the air with eyes calmly dissecting their plight. The Afghans thought of it as a distant cousin of the vulture.

An hour became a merciless day. And then another. And another, until several deadly days had almost passed.

Thor's leg by this had become infected. They wrapped it in strips of rag torn from one of the Afghan's loosely hanging strands of clothing.

The mid afternoon sun is usually the hottest. Its heat seemed to be deliberately assaulting them. The clothes of the guards were quickly distressed and shredded by the sharp anger of the countryside.

The men were caked in the desert dust as well. The Afghan clothing seemed to last better.

In the midst of the last day, the lost ones caught sight of the gnarled trunk of a Corkbark. The tree had suddenly appeared, like a half-opened fist in the desert's emptiness. The ancient *hakea suberia* was about nine metres tall and its shelter gave them some comfort.

The tree had ironically been for thousands of years a saviour to its indigenous guardians, curing sores and infections of the skin with its bark, and with its flowers providing a sweet-tasting drink. But for the desperate ones, it was simply shade.

Thor by this was in deep trouble. His leg, the one he had injured while kicking at the Afghans before the journey began, by now had the appearance of a sliver of rotting fruit. On top of this, he was sun-struck and deeply entrenched in exposure.

His face was black and his lips were fragments of broken pottery. Every breath was becoming a frantic struggle for survival. Heat, exhaustion and infection had taken possession of him. He was carried painfully for the last half mile up to the tree with the help of the very prisoners whose keeper he was.

Thor's fitter colleagues, were also becoming weak and losing their voices. By gesture they made the foreigners sit well away from them. The prisoners, in contrast, seemed calmly aware of what to do.

Ares and Mars focused their slits of eyes, squinting from their burnt, toasted faces, urgently and intently on Thor. They dared not look away. Time passed reluctantly.

The brief rest brought a few signs of recovery from the traumas of the long march. But not for Thor.

His condition grew rapidly worse. Every few minutes the other two Guards assessed his condition. The stricken sufferer groaned as he twisted with ever diminishing movements. He could speak only with great difficulty.

Finally, he seemed to yield, gave a faint shudder and became suddenly still. Mars leaned over and felt his pulse. He stiffened and looked at Ares.

Thor was dead.

They left the body where it lay. They had no strength or means to bury it.

An unnatural silence descended on the whole group. Each man shrank from the unspeakable harshness around him. The prisoners whispered to each other. They understood that the guard was killed by the land and not by them.

An odd change was suddenly discernible in their behaviour. They could see that the wheels of punishment were turning. Masters and underlings were suddenly equals.

Every one of them, guard and prisoner, was now a refugee, fleeing this time from the great, angry terrain itself.

And that particular adversary had a power which extended far beyond barbed wire and detention-house walls. The survivors, both friends and enemies, had no choice but to work together.

The living and the dead stayed under the tree until night came to set the living free. When the sun sank, they prepared to resume their trek, planning to make the most of the night's relief from the heat on their journey to nowhere.

Before leaving, they dragged Thor's body into the open for the next day's sun to begin its slow cremation. They left him to the bush and to its creatures of the ground and the air.

The fugitives stumbled on through the night. Morning slowly disentangled itself from the darkness, but they dared not stop. The faltering journey continued remorselessly into another day.

That one day seemed to merge into eternity. They trudged on through the next day. And the next.

Many more days passed. Until, amidst the apparent endlessness, hope seemed to be a ridiculous extravagance of mind.

Ares was still leading. He had noticed a clump of Weeping Pittosporum within relatively easy reach and decided to move towards it. These trees too could have provided balm for their injured limbs had they known what Aborigines know. Instead the cluster of trees brought another shattering demise.

Ares' mind was on shelter and perhaps moisture. As he approached the trees he quickened his steps a little in anticipation of a drink and shelter. Instead of shelter he was confronted by a demon.

Completely without warning, he found himself in the rearing presence of a massive Western Brown snake. He himself had long been aware of this snake. He knew that it was more toxic, if taunted, than a rattler or King Cobra. That is why terror gripped him when he saw it. He froze. He forgot to breathe.

Trapped between humans and a wall of trees and rock, the reptile had one option: to attack. The terrified guard felt suddenly naked and vulnerable. He saw nothing but the snake's lithe, rippling muscles, as it reared out of the undergrowth towards him, fangs flickering and laser eyes transfixing him. All the blood left Ares' face.

Flight had barely entered his head when the snake struck. He had never felt such pain before. It was as if his upraised arm had been severed.

The creature was a poisoned spear. It launched itself with impossible speed. It struck again. And again. The agony spread to his leg and to his thigh. He caught a brief, final blurred glimpse of the snake's long body as it majestically surged to freedom after the attack.

Weird lights flashed and flickered across the guard's eyes. A sudden darkness welled up from his body into his brain. Some of the others lifted him from the parched ground. He revived a little. Moaned a lot. They had no water to quench his parched lips. Before they could catch him, he fell again.

A little time passed. Mars tried to awaken his stricken colleague. He shook him. He slapped him.

He urged him into consciousness. The effort was futile. A coma descended upon him.

In less than an hour Ares was stiff and dead.

The survivors stood silent, looking at each other and the still body. The bush heard their silence. The trees nodded wisely like jurors passing final judgment. They chose to stay still, as if to re-establish their own style of world order.

No one spoke for a long time. Eventually, Mars struggled painfully to his feet. Eyes met. Glances travelled. Then the party moved off once more.

They left the second body where it had fallen.

The journey now had become an even greater torment. The principal sufferer was the last remaining Black Guard. Mars's comparatively vast body was now but a trace of its former self. His legs were failing and at times one foot lost track of the other. He fell many times.

Now captor and captives had completely reversed their roles in life. The guard was now in the care of the prisoners.

They struggled on. And on. Time was now a fiery monster, haunting them.

M1442 was the first to see an unpredictable variation in the landscape. That first sign was a wisp of dust scribbling on the horizon. It soon turned into one man riding a camel, with a train of several un- mounted beasts following behind him. The one-man caravan came towards the lost ones across the parched red plain.

Camels are strange, mysterious masters of the desert. They move with confident, relentless fluidity whatever their load, and whatever their destination. To the wretched wanderers this procession of living things possessed an eerie air of confidence and purpose. Above all, it brought immense relief.

The solitary figure astride the leading camel seemed to have authority over the world. He was Alaham, an almost legendary Afghan who had lived in the region for decades. First a workman on railroads and telegraph lines and now a solitary wanderer, he and his camels had traded for years imperiously across the vast inland desert.

His name today is known throughout the Northern Territory. He and his countrymen are one of the reasons the train, which bisects the continent, is named 'The Ghan.' This stranger, the adopted child of a foreign land, on that day was Zeus come down from Olympus.

By the time the two groups of desert wanderers met, Mars could barely walk and speak. He stretched one arm forward and then fell at the feet of the leading camel.

The solitary rider apparently chose not to speak in English. His words flowed fluently and animatedly in the Afghan tongue. The prisoners clustered around him listening intently and nodding to each other.

Now Mars was the outsider. He lay in the dust beneath the feet of the nearest camel while the creature stared dispassionately beyond the humans and methodically chewed its cud.

With an effort almost beyond human capacity, the stricken guard struggled to his feet. He steadied himself against the side of Alaham's camel.

'Water please! Water!' he croaked, but the stranger shook his head. Then the camel driver pointed towards the mountain range on the blurred horizon and mimed drinking. This was his way of explaining where water lay. Mars remained almost immobile, but the others moved with understanding.

More animated discussion followed. Alaham was powerful and authoritative as he looked down on them from his mount. He spoke again to the prisoners and gestured towards the other camels.

Two of his listeners painfully lifted Mars onto one of the beasts. Then the smallest outsider, M1441 who many days before and been battered for his sins by Mars, climbed onto the same beast with his persecutor and held him upright.

Swiftly and effortlessly, the remaining wanderers mounted. Skilfully they turned and headed for the hills. It was but a short journey, thanks to the energy of the willing beasts.

Soon the seven men found themselves at the base of the mountain range that loomed arrogantly above them. The hills were steep in places, clothed in trees, and unexpectedly shrouded in a soothing mist.

Far above, with the help of the sun, the fugitives could see a clear stream flashing between ancient rocks.

The climb to salvation was not easy. Alaham barked instructions to the other Afghans. They half pushed, half carried their ailing keeper towards the stream which rippled and babbled invitingly, mercifully a little way above them.

It took the men a long time to reach the water. There were many stumbles. Eventually they found the mountain stream at their feet. They buried their bodies in its coolness. The camel driver stood back watching the others drink. He was in no hurry.

That time passed almost happily. Many birds twittered in the trees, noisily exchanging information about the intruders.

Mars began to recover. With help, he got to his feet. His eyes offered thanks. He mumbled gratitude and squeezed one of the helpful arms.

He looked around him taking renewed stock of the location. He began to think that there might be a way out of this mire after all. He must find a new pathway to survival.

Civilisation lay across this range. Unsteadily he let his eyes follow the stream. He began to walk, all the while looking towards the horizon. Two of the Afghans tracked him at a distance.

It would have been easy for the prisoners to over-power him. But they were thoughtful, kind men who had learned the value of order and respect for the rule of law--even if the law itself was marked by occasional flaws.

He looked back at them. What was this?

What was happening to the world he once knew? He could see in the other men's eyes a strange forgive-ness. An unexpected caring. Quirky and novel thoughts were moving around his brain.

If he survived this ordeal, he would not be the same man. There were things he could do in that refugee camp. Things he must do.

But his first task was to organise survival now.

'Where exactly is our pathway? ' thought Mars. He stretched his battered body to extend his gaze.. He was feeling stronger now. A little stronger. He stopped and listened to the swishing of the water.

A practical man, he decided he needed to plot his escape route through the valley. To be lost again would be disastrous.

He could hear what sounded like a waterfall close by. Carefully he followed the stream towards what might be a better view of the pathway to safety.

A few minutes later he found himself breathless before a vast panorama. From the awesome heights where he stood, his eyes seemed to be those of eagles.

Not far away, the stream took a leap over a jagged edge and turned into a waterfall, tumbling gently into a deep valley. There below him, beyond the waterfall, Mars could see a white track trailing into the valley's distance.

And there, on the horizon, was the smoke of a city. Yes, that was his way back from the abyss. His old verve and energy were coming back.

.

He swung his head to look at the two Afghans behind him. A smile flirted with his lips. In a devious way, something more than mere forgiveness was beginning to find a place in his mind.

The old iron of his world view had rusted away. In its place was the gentleness of standing in other people's shoes; of feeling other people's pain; and at last understanding. A new era was dawning. When he returned to the prison, he would work to bring changes for the refugees.

'Now. That way, past the big rock, is our best route,' he thought. He stood for a moment, simply looking into the distance. 'Yes. That is the way we must go.'

As his eyes rediscovered the horizon, something moved unexpectedly. He felt a tremor beneath his feet. The barest shudder. Then the earthly scaffolding beneath the rock on which he stood gave way.

M1441 saw the danger before anyone else. He lunged forward in a desperate bid to save the guard. To catch him before he fell.

He failed, and his fingertips faintly touched the outstretched hands of his former master. Their eyes met.

Then Mars, the jailer, was gone.

The forgiving, caring eyes he had once blackened, now were part of the last human face he ever saw.

He fell like a wounded swan, tumbling and screaming, after grasping desperately at wildflowers and prickly bushes that came away in his hands.

Past the blur of green and grey of the hanging gums he plunged. Into the cool emptiness of space. Beyond the waterfall, towards the sharp edged rocks which he knew, in that final fleeting falling, were waiting for him below.

He was a big man still. He hit the base of the cliff with a muffled thud and died at once.

Once more the land had fashioned its own justice. The wheels of anger had at last stopped turning.

Yet again an eerie silence fell upon the living.

Those who did not fall could not move or speak. Each simply stood with downcast eyes focused on the body below. Now only outsiders were left. They stood together above the chasm of death.

When the camel-driver spoke, the stillness seemed glad to be broken. The chatter returned, generating a strange air of purpose. It was time to leave this place forever.

If you had been there after the descent from the mountain, you would have seen six men, confidently mounted on camels, riding in a stately line to somewhere beyond the setting sun of that day. Where that may have been I do not know.

* * * * *

Almost a decade after the events I have described, a large, elegantly black Rolls Royce swept into the internment-centre, after crossing the rugged land-scape from the coast. This vehicle would have made that long journey over that rough, barely defined road with air-conditioned ease.

A foreign flag fluttered significantly from its bonnet. This was clearly a visit of official status. The First Secretary of a Diplomatic Mission was ushered by his chauffeur from the vehicle. He was met by the leaders of the establishment.

To my surprise, after almost an hour, I was summoned with several other older prisoners into the diplomat's presence. I was impressed by the compassion of his glances and the diplomatic assurance of his manner.

We talked softly together for some time. He told me a story of the desert. We spoke too of other things, especially of changes taking place in the world of politics. And then he left us.

That dignitary knew this place. He spoke confidently in perfect, though accented English. He himself, as a young man, had worn a number devised by this establishment. He was in fact, Number M1441.

Ares and Mars and Thor are now but faint memories in this place, my Laura.

With love,

Narni.

* * * * *

XIII

All Is Not Fair
in Love and War

The way to heaven is the same in every place
— Diogenes

Dearest Laura,
Who Is Always In My Mind,

Something was different this morning. I had my usual fleeting moment of complete despair when I awoke.

This world was bleaker than yesterday's world when I struggled from my bed. Hope could not be found anywhere in my mind. So I struck the wall first with my fist and then my head. The wall was not damaged. There is no wisdom in giving to yourself a sore head.

Today I have another story to tell. It was told to me by a friend in the exercise yard, M1030. He was so sad here. He longed in vain for the comfort of kindness. I think I gave him some, but only through words and the willingness to listen.

He told me this story just a few days before he became very ill and was taken away. I believe he is dead.

It is a tale of recent times. A tale of his daughter, who was once a flower-seller in a distant land, a land torn completely apart by war.

His daughter was more beautiful than a spring morning, or a bird on the wing or a dewdrop sparkling on a spider's web, he said. She was young and vibrant, in love with every day and with her work as a flower-seller in the village square.

Every morning she would hurry lightly to a tiny stall, pulling her little cart of flowers and set up for her day of selling. Each sale would bring a smile and kind words for the departing buyer and somehow make the scent of the flowers sweeter. It was a happy life that flowed like pleasant music.

Until one benighted day, when sudden discord came to the square. Its form was gunfire. Just a spasmodic staccato at first with fitful thunderous background rumbles. The people around her paused and listened. They turned their heads in the direction of the sounds. On the horizon, smoke began to rise.

Gradually the sounds grew louder. People hurried away. The flower girl stayed.

Soon the gunfire became a crescendo. Louder. Still louder. Then Hell invaded the square. There was a deafening roar amidst smoke and the stench of burning. There was a blast. The girl felt herself lifted and pushed by irresistible force across the street. She fell like a cast off doll into the dust.

For a time she lost awareness.

If she had been awake she would have heard the sound of running feet. More crackling of gunfire. Shouts and cries of pain. Orders in a strange language. Then brief silence.

Slowly consciousness returned. Dimly she noticed a foreign shadow falling over her. Looking down at her was a young man in an exotic uniform. Then she made out a face that showed more concern than hostility. She felt two warm hands lifting her gently to her feet.

Eyes met. Suddenly two strong arms lifted her and she felt herself carried swiftly through the smoke and noise away from the chaos. In a very short time she found herself sitting on a seat in what seemed to be a safe place.

She looked at the soldier. She knew he was her enemy. Yet there was no animosity in his face. He was so young. Care seemed to shine from him as their eyes met again.

He offered her some water from his flask. She took it gladly. She began to feel human again. Life was returning.

He stayed with her a little while. They had no words but somehow, just for that short time, they did not need them.

She noticed a wisp of fair hair under his helmet. There were freckles on his cheeks and his eyes were mysteriously blue. He noticed the black ringlets of hair touching her forehead, the deep darkness of her eyes. And he would not forget her lips.

The flower girl knew her words to her saviour were meaningless, but nevertheless she softly said, 'Thank you,' and smiled at him. He looked into those gentle, dark eyes reassuringly.

The flower girl softly stretched out her hard to touch his arm. He responded by gently reaching out to her hand and then enfolding it in his own. He came closer until their lips almost touched. They kissed.

It was a fleeting kiss. She withdrew against her wishes.

They stayed very close to each other. Clocks seemed suddenly to have stopped. They lingered until a loud cry came from nearby.

He stiffened. Turned to her and magically, for a moment they were entwined in each other's arms. Then he squeezed her hand, spun around and was gone. Although still surrounded by others, each felt a sudden loneliness.

The girl stayed there, bemused. The tumult slowly died. So did the day. In the reassuring, fading light she hurried home to her family as rapidly as her bruises would allow.

* * * * *

Time began to pass again. The war appeared to be elsewhere. But she remembered her friendly enemy. At different times during the day his smile would come back into her mind.

Once again she would feel the warmth of his hand. And his body. It was a strange and unexpected comfort.

Slowly order came back into her life. The square recovered itself and people moved freely once again preoccupied with life.

The flowers and the girl returned to the village square. A flower is not the fleeting thing it seems to be. No other living thing returns love with such passion. Its beauty is kept safe in the very seeds that accompany its destruction, and so lasts forever. Not so with humans.

The flower seller's sales continued for some months. So did her smiles. Existence once more seemed to resemble life in a garden.

Until the war returned.

It all happened again. The gunfire came back to shatter the tranquility. Noises and rumblings approached.

Chaos this time came quickly. The shouting and the screams left little need for other warnings.

But now the girl had the alertness of experience. She quickly gathered her flowers and her cart, and ran away with frightened legs.

Through a side street, down a hill and across a park she sped, her footsteps keeping time with her beating heart. She began to believe she would escape unharmed this time. And then with a gasp of trepidation, she stopped.

She had stumbled into the crossfire of a bitter street battle. The smell of danger was everywhere. Wherever she looked, broken concrete lay around her. Bullets thumped on everything. Shock waves of sound ran around her frightened brain. She crouched in the shadows, motionless with fear. There she stayed.

Eventually the conflict eased. She decided to move to a safer place.

Slowly she started to walk across the cluttered fractured street. She cautiously picked her way through wreckage and the bodies lying in distorted postures like drunken revellers at the end of an orgy. Occasional ricochets reminded her of danger.

She paused in the middle of a step with a shudder of surprise and horror. There at her feet was her benefactor of such a brief time ago.

His eyes were open without seeing and his hands, those soft and warm and kind hands, were twisted in the aftermath of pain.

The flower girl stood motionless for some time. She gave an almost inaudible gasp. Tears came unannounced to her eyes. A strange emptiness seemed suddenly to have confiscated her world.

Then she quickly bent down and closed the eyes. She reached out and touched the hands. Perhaps she imagined it, but her touch seemed to change the rigour of mortis into the warmth and softness she had previously known.

She turned after what seemed forever, suddenly possessed with the desire to flee from this mise en scène of Death. Too late.

Her sadness was destined not to last. There was no anticipation, no warning for the flower girl. Death came instantly. Bullets, on their mission to kill, do not discriminate. Flesh is flesh and bone is bone and we die when a bullet hits them, whoever we are.

She was struck before she could move even one step away from the dead soldier. She fell across his body, her open eyes still seemingly aware of the caring enemy.

A few droplets of the blood from her white dress found their way onto the uniform that covered the soldier's once warm and comforting arms. The two lay there together for a long time in their lifeless embrace.

Peace eventually came to the scene. The pavements were washed and tidiness returned. To the children of tomorrow who walked along that street, it would seem but an ordinary, uneventful place.

Sleep well my love. May the beautiful leaves of your life be green and then turn golden with age.

M1030 has gone now forever from this place.

Narni.

* * * * *

A flower is not the fleeting thing it seems to be. No other living thing returns love with such passion. Its beauty is kept safe in the very seeds that accompany its destruction, and so lasts forever. Not so with humans.

XIV

Tout Passe

Acta est fibula
The drama has been acted out.
 — Augustus Caesar, just before he died

Dearest Laura,
The Link In My Chain,

Here I remain still . . . an outsider sharing life with demonised others. Yet what mystic beauty I have found among these feared outsiders!

But now my time has come. This is my last letter to you. M0131 is about to pay allegiance to silence once again. To put down his pen.

I nearly died yesterday. There were pains in my body, especially my heart. Perhaps it is broken. But it is still beating today.

It has been a long life. So many follies to observe. O what a mangled mess is man! The only creature which smokes, uses words as weapons, kills members of its own species unseen, and systematically destroys its own nest.

Yet here I have shared in the lives of the generalised others. They have taught me things. Better things.

This experience has changed me. Even you now, dearest Laura, would possibly not recognise me as the man you once knew, should we meet again. I am even a stranger now to myself.

But not to love.

Love is everywhere. The trouble is it is hidden behind or under heaps of angry stones. Under broken walls. Or behind shibboleths of danger. Yet it remains triumphant as our only defence against hate. We have to give it time to succeed.

Ah time! As I count the last shadows in this place, I realise that my old friend Ovid was right when he said time devours things. It has no superiors. No controllers. It is the one truth we can never deny.

Time. Time. Time.

The same old enemy, yet, in a last friendly gesture it will be a friend, to shepherd you triumphantly away from despair and into peace. It is our last resort. The tincture for all wounds. The last panacea for all sadness.

My days have withered into months and years in this prison. Here I am, the concocted foe of my captors. Yet I can never be the adversary they seek.

That is because, my dear child, I have no ill will towards them now, only pity. Even though they have hammered me into silence and tormented me into wakefulness.

I have even had to hide my words lest they chew them up. At times I have longed for even my thoughts to disappear. But, after all this, still I cannot hate.

Ah Laura! Perhaps pain is a hallucinogen. Did I imagine it all?

Am I too, such stuff as dreams are made on? Were my friends ever really here? Or were they no more than my foolish fancy?

Never mind. It does not matter. I need no answer. I have learnt here that ordinary people are not always as frail as they may seem. Their lives may not be mundane trivialities.

Instead, perhaps they can leave the earth and take possession of the sky. Fly amongst the clouds to seize the voiceless moon and shake it out of its ageless silence so that it tells us what it really sees.

That moon is shining on me now through my little window, changing my cell into ubiquity. Thoughts are everything. Now I am ready to leave this barren place. How, I do not know.

Am I really a dangerous man? In the Country of the Blind, a rose is a weed because of its thorns. Perhaps they will kill me. But we shall see.

The darkness of night does not last forever. My mind is touched by the imprisoned lightning of the Statue of Liberty, Mother of Exiles, set free in my dreams from the sea-washed, sunset gates of far New York to reach around the world.

But my last thoughts are for the forgotten ones who have been sent from this desert of disdain to despair and death too many lives ago. No more keeping quiet for me. No more. No more. That is why I write. Some day, these words of mine may be read. Even by you.

Goodbye my dearest child of tomorrow. My pen is about to be still

M0131 will soon be gone forever from this place.

Narni.

* * * * *

THE SUN: I am sorry. Vast powers, beyond my control, have made me cross your boundaries and set here in your land.

BORDER CONTROL OFFICER: But have you filled in the necessary forms?

— *S. J. Cavell*

* * * * *

Epilogue

THE LETTER FROM DOCTOR MUSTIKOS

Dr Samuel Cavell
CEO Editing
Universal Publishing
Circular Quay, Sydney
New South Wales, 2000, Australia

4 July 2004

Dear Dr Cavell

I write in a state of profound amazement. I have just completed my reading of your first edition of *Letters To Nowhere*. It is almost impossible for me to describe my feelings at this moment, but I shall do my best.

That reading, Dr Cavell, has changed my life. You see, I believe that I am the Laura of the text. I further believe that the letters were written by my father, Dr Andreus Mustikos. The evidence is overwhelming.

There are so many personal references, and the style is his. 'Narni' was my special name for him. This, my letter to you, because of my sudden awareness of the situation, has had priority over my food and sleep.

My father is, or possibly was, an astonishing, enigmatic man. Emeritus Professor of Cultural Difference at a major Australian university whose name at this stage does not matter.

His wife had died in my infancy and I was his only child. He was my counsel, my guardian, my mentor and my inspiration. Without him I would have virtually ceased to exist.

Yet this man, my loving father, was a strange one. Manic impressive. He was an extrovert. A showman. He wore oddly elegant, brightly coloured clothes in his normal working day.

He did not smoke or drink, fornicate, lie or cheat. Yet he understood human frailties better than any other person I have ever known.

He had, as was the accepted convention, climbed up the university status ladder through political allegiances and petty alliances with powerful influences. He had published profusely, travelled abroad to status-filled conferences and astutely dropped research findings into journals and the pigeonholes of sensation-seeking journalists. Relentlessly he rose towards senior administrative power.

Then, at the crest of his wave of acceptability, his world abruptly changed. The lightning of under-standing suddenly made him as angry as Hell. This anger grew because he came to realise that the world he had devoted his life to was robbed of its innocence. He began to look around him with different eyes and he did not like what he saw.

His lectures became revolutionary speeches--declarations of war against hypocrisy. Against doing unto others what you won't let them do unto you. These lectures were startling and disturbingly interesting. They would constantly attract hordes of outsiders from unrelated faculties and beyond the university. There were never any empty seats.

He spared no fools in his tirades. He used to say jokingly to me, "You must never lecture in somebody else's sleep." Nobody ever dozed within earshot of him and the favourite theme of his discourse was: human stupidity.

Greed was another object of his scorn. Usury, he would declare, was once a sin until the widow's mite was invested and became the mogul's might. Now everything has a price and shareholders are the chosen people. To Hell with the poverty, starvation and death of the needy.

He would rant against the compliant Press as weapons of mass instruction on false causes. He was proud too, of his enemies who attacked him often. He seemed to be eternally angry, and yet he would give his last meal to the needy and his last breath to the suffering.

His students loved him and the university tolerantly respected him because of his drawing capacity in the newly commercialised market for students. In the dawning era of bums-on-seats funding, he was valuable property. In spite of his radicalism, he was promoted. The ultimate highest academic office was his for the taking.

But, in his case, ultimate war was inevitable.

There was hellfire in his eventual dispute with the university. He resigned his post more than ten years ago.

The scene was his inauguration as Pro-Vice Chancellor.

It was a glowing ceremony, replete with *Gaudeamus Igitur*, an academic procession that made peacocks look drab and dowdy, a sonorous choir and a healthy audience with the usual routine media attachment.

It was to be his golden moment.

Expectation filled the air of the ceremony. People leant forward when he approached the lectern to speak. What a surprise they were in for!

My father's speech rocked the ivy halls and brought their walls of indifference crumbling to the ground. I have used notes he left behind to reconstruct his words.

Your Excellency, Vice Chancellor, Members of Council, Distinguished Guests, Ladies and Gentlemen,

Much have I have travelled in the realms of academe. For many years have I pondered upon why one should belong to a university. I think of the word *universe* from the Latin *universus* implying 'turned into one.'

That is what I understand a university is. A unity. A community if you like, where ideas are shared without fear or retribution, for as long as the music of existence lasts.

I think of true scientific principles, where cover up is inconceivable. I think of the freedom to share triumphs of the mind and to criticise them without penalty. I think of conclusions drawn purely on the basis of valid and reliable evidence. I think of the safety that lies in this world of thought, because of the power of integrity.

But what do I find instead, in this petty little world of self-interest? Degeneration. Ruin. Decomposition.

That's right. You heard me. There is not just one rotten apple in this academic barrel. It's the barrel itself where the trouble lies. That pathetic, flimsy container is about to fall apart.

The Ivory Tower has become the Tower of Babel.

Look around you. Open your eyes. What is happening here? Look at education--our X-ray of the future.

Why, in wisdom's name, is learning penalised by the imposition of vast costs on the learners. Study dependent on mortgages that can take a lifetime to repay for every graduate. Why do we ignore the immense economic returns society gains from a well-educated person, in any human field?

Why do we tolerate these present obscene study debts imposed on students by men whose degrees cost them nothing? What do our wise professors have to say about this?

Where is everybody?

And what about research, the lifeblood and heartbeat of every university? What a sick joke it is today! Research that has no financial strings attached? No agendas? No conditions for funding such as profit or political favours? Research whose only allegiance is to truth? Where is it?

Where is everybody?

What of the wars against humanity in Iraq and Afghanistan and other places? It is a war-crime to kill innocent civilians. Persecution and terror tactics must not be condoned. But you approve of them with your silence. Who are the terrorists?

Where is everybody?

If such well-known insurgents as Mahatma Gandhi, Emile Zola or Woodrow Wilson were lecturing here, they would be sacked.

Where is everybody?

And why are student unions emasculated into poverty. Fees abandoned. Are we afraid of young minds? Because our youths are more likely to speak the truth and name our follies, must we quake in our boots?

Alas and alack we must all watch our back!

The accepted conspiracies of suppression supported by you the élite, defy comprehension. Where are the voices of healthy debate in these universities, our ancient castles of truth?

Silent. The lack of sound is deafening!

Metternich and the Carlsbad Decrees are alive and well now.

Now! Now! Now!

And what about protecting the environment with the atomic bullshit? We are so blind to nuclear pollution that we cannot even pronounce it correctly.

Where is everybody?

Where is the wisdom of fairness, learned friends and others, in this university. Of all places on earth, a university is the one where inhuman acts anywhere in the world: lies, prejudice, imprisonment without trial, torture and tyranny--should be exposed, hung, drawn and quartered.

Yes. I know some of you speak up as individuals. But where is the unified institutional voice? Gone to bow to political or corporate masters, or to singing practice for the national anthem!

Where is everybody?

And worst of all. Blackest of all your sins, darker than any devised by evildoers since someone told the very first lie, is your willingness to let flight in boats from horror and fear and mental destruction be called a crime. There is no such thing as a queue to escape from atrocity, savagery and hideous outrage.

There are no choices. There are no choices. You are all slaves of globalisation. What moves is money. And power. But never people to freedom. That is a nuisance.

I speak not for myself, but for the countless oppressed of today and tomorrow who have no voice. That is why I have no compunction in telling you to stick your sense of justice up your arses. Because that sense is so small, I know that it would in no way interfere with your bodily processes.

That is why, dear friends, you have just heard my last speech. This is why I am about to quit this port for ever. This place is no longer my place.

Goodbye. I leave it all to you.

With that, Doctor Cavell, my father left the stage as the congregation recoiled in simmering amazement. As he hurried away, he began disrobing. First, he flung his academic cap high into the crowded hall. Then his hood.

Then he dropped his gown to the floor behind him as he hurried down the steps of the stage. Next, the coat of his suit was tossed beneath a row of seats as he passed. Then came his tie, which he ripped from his throat and threw away so that it swept and wriggled through the air like a protest streamer caught in the winds of change.

By this, he had almost left the building, leaving behind him a dizzy silence. He stamped his way along most of the red carpet leading from the stage to the Great Hall's capacious entrance. A few moments more and he was gone.

This careful planner, despite his madcap demeanour, had hidden a bicycle behind a hedge outside the Great Hall. As I joined the crush of the bewildered audience suddenly running after him, I realised we would not catch him.

You no doubt remember all this. It was in the news for a while, wasn't it?

My last vision of my father was of a determinedly crouched figure, peddling furiously out of the university grounds and into the safety of distance. I have not seen him since.

When I arrived home I found, on my bed, a briefcase containing all the papers needed to secure my acquisition of his property and certain funds. As well, there was a single rose with a card that read:

> To My Darling Laura,
> Love Always,
> Narni.

There was a whirlpool of discord for a while after he left, in my heart and in the minds of others. His actions actually, did not cause great surprise among some of his colleagues. There was a tendency to laugh it off. After all, this was Mustikos, the well-known iconoclast.

It was his typical way of replacing a whimper with a bang. Despite a few flickers from journalists' tongues, as a subject of discussion, he faded away quite quickly.

His lawyers helped by attributing his actions to mental fatigue and a decision to take early retirement. My father's place in the university was quickly declared vacant.

Cunningly, he had written in advance to his closest colleagues indicating intentions of resignation followed by further studies in The United States. Thus his absence attracted little attention for some time and finally was not noticed any more. Fatalities and scandals were drawing attention to more interesting people.

Now Dr Cavell, my father and I were very close and knew each other's thoughts well. We had often discussed death and agreed that for final departure of any kind, a swift and clean break was always best.

As soon as I found that rose on my bed, I knew that he had decided to leave for good the world we both had known. As for his colleagues; when, despite a few raised eyebrows, he did not appear after several years, it was widely assumed he was either dead or had migrated.

To me, after this final catharsis, came complete understanding of the pain and disgust he had endured for so long.

In the light of these letters, I feel I am in a position wisely to guess at my father's movements since our last day together. At that time of disintegration, before news fully reached public circles, he probably boarded a plane for a Third World destination. Speed of departure would have been important, and was no doubt planned in advance.

When he arrived in his new world, he undoubtedly changed his identity and I am certain destroyed his passport. We can only guess about his activities after that. I am sure he would have used his skills to improve the society around him.

Language would have been no problem. He spoke several.

He was also good with his hands as well as his mind. I can imagine him doing physical labour, changing his own general appearance and sharing ideas widely.

I can also imagine him deciding on life in a war-torn country and I believe he would, when confronted with injustice, have become an insurgent. He has always been a voice for the vast hordes of underprivileged people in the world, especially the children.

I have been thinking too, that world events would not have escaped him. That has given me a crazy idea.

What if he had heard of the scandals relating to refugees that are now part of this country's history. The queue-jumping fallacies and the unjust or illegal deportation. I know he would have been very angry about the patent dishonesty and cruelty he saw.

What if he had decided, as a true academic, to do some action research and come back himself as a refugee? To place himself with the last of his money on a boat among the dreaded boat-people and truly share their existence?

It would have been easy for him to hide his identity. After all, he is, or was, an outcast in his own country. He was for much of his past, a warrior with a very sharp mind.

I know that mind. My suggestion is just the kind of thing he would do. I believe he has done it.

I know too, he would have thought of this as a way to reveal to the world undisclosed qualities of internment life and I am sure he would have predicted the finding of the letters by the one guard he knew well.

But it may have got away on him. Perhaps he ran into insurmountable challenges. Was conquered by them.

And now my heart aches. What if his true identity was discovered in that centre? What if they found him out, feared him and gave him the CIA treatment? He is a perfect candidate for extraordinary rendition.

Or what if the pain and frustration of everything finally caught up with him, became too much and drove him in the end to take his own life? It is possible. This uncertainty is leading me to considerable anguish.

I have one faint hope in spite of the evidence. What if, in defiance of the circumstances, he has been set free by a Samaritan administrator with the aid of a whistle-blower? We have little choice sometimes, but to live with whatever hope we can find.

I am afraid I see no immediate solution to my agony. If my father is dead, Dr Cavell, ask not for whom the bell tolls. It tolls for me. And yet, perhaps as in my dreams, his footsteps have led him beyond the desert towards the hopeful heartbeat of a friendly city, somewhere. Somewhere.

To conclude this, I have attached a poem that my father wrote and shared with me some years ago.

Regards,

Laura Mustikos

*****

Paths of Pity

Can you see the stranger in that isolated room
Writhing in the wreckage of his futile days,
Empty eyes of misery, expression without a face,
A melancholic vagrant in an alien sun's disgrace?

O why do you claim that you're always right
And say that for you a reason's there?
Let me wander with you, along the Paths of Pity
And we'll discover mortal mischief lying every-
where.

Can you see his lonely child in another place,
Lingering through the sorrows of a family lost,
Walking past, without a word and no face left to
greet,
Searching alone for a broken home along a broken
street?

O why do you claim that you're always right
And say that for you a reason's there?
Let me wander with you, along the Paths of Pity
And we'll discover mortal mischief lying every-
where.

Can you see that soldier outside that shattered
building
Listening for the sounds that once were there,

Looking for an enemy, ready for the fray,
Finding only silent ruins with nothing left to say?

O why do you claim that you're always right
And say that for you a reason's there?
Let me wander with you, along the Paths of Pity
And we'll discover mortal mischief lying every-
where.

In that crowded cell-block at a quarter past doom
Can you see the lonely light flickering in the gloom,
Swinging from the ceiling like a terrified eye
Sharing in the torment of a hostile, foreign sky?

O why do you claim that you're always right
And say that for you a reason's there?
Let me wander with you, along the Paths of Pity
And we'll discover mortal mischief lying every-
where.

* * * * *

Coda

Some Of My Favourite Refugees

A Personal Selection

Tan Le 1978

Young Australian of the Year in 1998, Tan Le is the daughter of boat people. Her family fled Vietnam in 1981 and spent five days in a little boat before they were rescued by a British oil tanker and taken to a Malaysian refugee camp. They spent some months there until, with compassion, Australia welcomed them as refugees.

They had no possessions and scant knowledge of English when they arrived here. They joined no fictitious queue and had no evidence of economic benefit to Australia. But they had Tan Le. Largely thanks to a mother who worked and studied English to help educate her children, Tan Le gained entry to university at the age of 16.

She was awarded an accounting Scholarship in 1997 and graduated with a Commerce and Law degree with honours from Monash University in 1998. She became a barrister and solicitor in early 2000, and has spent her young, adult life helping underprivileged refugees and native born, as a brilliant entrepreneur.

Frédéric Chopin 1810-1849

A gifted refugee, whose body lies in Paris and whose heart rests in the Church of the Holy Cross in Warsaw. Chopin, friend of Charles Dickens and object of Queen Victoria's admiration, spent his brief and brilliant adult life in exile from Poland, fighting the Russian possession of his homeland through his music.

Li Lu 1966

Student hero of the Tiananmen Square demonstrations of 1989, Li Lu, a former refugee, has now become a successful component of American society.

A brilliant scholar, child of activists in his homeland, he achieved the unique distinction of being awarded three degrees from Columbia University on the one day, in 1996. Now an icon of the American capitalist system, he will long be remembered for the humanity he inspired in another country, his own.

Albert Einstein 1879-1955

Einstein, the genius who failed his first entrance exam for engineering in Zurich, proved among other things the folly of using a single examination to judge human beings. Because of early failures, he was at first employed as a mere technical expert third class at the Berne patent office. Time ensured his relativity to greatness, and the Nobel Prize for Physics in 1921.

His flight to America from the Nazis helped him become yet another refugee who rose to great heights. We all know why.

He was a fighter for causes too, auctioning his 1905 paper on relativity to help the war effort of 1944, raising $6 million, and later aiding Bertrand Russell's anti nuclear movement. Although the Manhattan Project, which did in fact produce the first truly frightening evidence of E=MC2, the atomic bomb, caused him much later anguish, it was promoted by Einstein to forestall the Nazis and Japanese.

Rudolph Nureyev 1938-1993
A real queue jumper. Actually he made a famous leap over the barrier at Le Bourget airport, France, on June 17, 1961 to seek political asylum.

A passionate ballet virtuoso, he was born of Muslim, peasant parents into a challenging, Russian existence. He was 23 at the time of that barrier leap in France, and already a Russian star. When he fled, he entered a new world of stardom on stage and film, in the company of such Western stars as Dame Margot Fonteyn, and had a brilliant directing and teaching career as well.

He remained a wanderer for the rest of his life, to the benefit of countless fans, many of whom remain today in the country which he originally left behind.

Bob Marley 1945-1981

Robert Nesta Marley, "Bob", was one of the great voices of the underprivileged in the twentieth century. A Rastafarian, born into the former slave colony of Jamaica, he became a powerful political force for the underprivileged, especially the ghetto youth on his island, through his music and activism.

So powerful was this recipient of the UN Peace Medal, that on the eve of a free peace concert he was about to give in Kingston, gunmen invaded his home and wounded him and his wife. He spent much of his short life facing up to danger and escaping from it. No time for queues for this refugee.

Thomas Mann 1875-1955

Another refugee Nobel Prize winner, this time for literature in 1929. Thomas Mann was one of the most powerful critics of Nazism in his native land.

He sought refuge in Switzerland and then America, where his fame and activism grew until the xeno-phobic hysteria of Joseph McCarthy made him a refugee again. He became a Swiss citizen in 1953, two years before he died.

Max Born 1882-1970

A life-long friend of Albert Einstein and a fellow Nobel Prize winner: in 1954 for Physics, Max Born is another German refugee. He has surprising and special links with Australia.

Although he had Jewish parents, he became a Lutheran when he married Hedwig in 1913. One of the children of this marriage was Irene, who was to marry Brin Newton-John and give Australia a British-born entertainment star, Olivia.

To the Nazis, when Hitler came to power in 1933, Born was still a Jew. So he fled Germany to continue his brilliant scientific and academic life in England. The advent of this alien was of immense value to the University of Cambridge, the University of Edinburgh, and the many brilliant Ph D students he supervised. Among his many lifetime achievements were the development of quantum mechanics and major contributions to solid-state physics and optics.

The Max Born prize, sponsored by the German Physical Society by and the British Institute of Physics, is awarded annually.

Victor Hugo 1802-1885
Victor-Marie Hugo, French poet, playwright, novelist, essayist, artist, important French statesman, human rights activist and Romantic, was almost a perpetual refugee.

He fled from the dictator Louis Napoleon (Napoleon III) who seized complete power over parliament in 1851, to Brussels, then Jersey, and finally settled with his family on the channel island of Guernsey at Hauteville House, where he would live in exile until 1870.

He was famous for many reasons--a prolific artist and poet, as well as a still vastly popular novelist. *Les Misérables* and *Notre-Dame de Paris* (known in English also as *The Hunchback of Notre-Dame*), are still part of our modern existence on this side of the world. His presence in England made him an influence on Dickens' social conscience, and even on Queen Victoria's attitude to capital punishment. He also influenced Camus and Dostoevsky.

His experience of exile may have inspired these words of his, so relevant to today:

> Amnesty is as good for those who give it
> as for those who receive it. It has the
> admirable quality of bestowing mercy on
> both sides.

Peter Lorre 1904-1964

As Ladislav Lowenstein, he became a refugee in Romania, Austria and finally America, where he became known as the much-loved film star, Peter Lorre. He was a wonderful shady character in such movies as *The Maltese Falcon* and *Casablanca*.

During the McCarthy witch-hunts, he was asked if he knew any other shady characters. He replied by naming everyone he had ever met. They left him alone after that. Sometimes fools can be exposed if we carry their behaviour to its logical conclusion.

Travel well, and may every arrival bring you joy.

— Royce Levi

The Author

Royce Levi has been a teacher for more than 50 years, teaching in one-teacher, infants, primary and secondary schools, and in universities. He has a BA degree from Newcastle University, a Masters degree in Education from the University of New South Wales, and a Masters degree in English Literature from the University of Sydney. He began serious writing on his retirement in 2004.

He is now the author of four books whose subjects range between politics, poetry and the history of cricket. This novella, *Letters to Nowhere*, is currently being made into a feature Australian film.

He regards writing as one of the great adventures of life and freely admits he is yet to master its subtle mysteries. His life as a teacher has brought him far more joy than anguish. He sees teaching not as an injection of knowledge from on high, but as a shared journey of learning with anyone who chooses to join him.

* * * * *

This text is a work of fiction. Any resemblance to real persons, living or dead, or to real places, is pure coincidence, with the exceptions of the photographs and Coda, which are used with respect and goodwill as illustrations of the main themes of the book.

CPSIA information can be obtained at www.ICGtesting.com
Printed in the USA
LVOW080041251112

308651LV00007B/298/P